MOVIE TIME Social Learning

Using Movies to Teach Social Thinking® and Social Understanding

ANNA VAGIN, PhD

Social Thinking Publishing, Santa Clara, California
www.socialthinking.com

Movie Time Social Learning
Using Movies to Teach Social Thinking® and Social Understanding

Anna Vagin, PhD

Library of Congress Control Number: 2012951166

ISBN: 978-0-9825231-9-3

Social Thinking Publishing
404 Saratoga Avenue, Suite 200
Santa Clara, CA 95050
Phone: (408) 557-8595
Fax: (408) 557-8594

This book was printed and bound in the United States by Think, Inc.
TSP is a sole source provider of Social Thinking products in the U.S.
Books may be purchased online at www.socialthinking.com

Dedication

To my mother, Irene Wogak Vagin, who passed her love of writing to me, and my father, Veniamin Feodorovich Vagin, who, through his example, taught me the power of not giving up, and taking everything "po tihonku" (bit by bit).

Acknowledgments

First, I'd like to express my great appreciation to the children and families with whom I work. Your efforts and affection make it a true pleasure to come to work every day, and I'm deeply grateful for all you continue to teach me.

My wonderful family has been there to move me along this multi-year process. My very loving husband, Bruce Heller, provided invaluable and honest editing, always an eager discussion partner no matter the time or place. My son Jake received many fewer baked treats than he deserved and was always there to help with my never-ending technical glitches. My daughter Carly supported me "hands on," keyboarding with the speed of a racehorse, as well as emotionally, always expressing her confidence in me.

I have had many amazing teachers in my life who formed my thinking, including Carol Prutting, PhD, who always pushed beyond the status quo; Adrianna Schuler, PhD, the smiling brilliance on my dissertation and orals committee; Anne Fernald, PhD, who taught me to look to the beginnings of relationships; and of course, Michelle Winner, Pam Crooke, and Stephanie Madrigal, whose work has pushed the field of Social Thinking far.

Thanks also to Sue Barnett, Veronica Zysk, and Sandy Horwich at Social Thinking Publishing, all of whom helped me to organize (and shorten) my ideas.

CONTENTS

ANNA VAGIN, PhD
MOVIE TIME
Social Learning
CD
Contents
Lesson Plans
Visual Aids and Templates
Letters and Forms
© 2012 ANNA VAGIN
Social Thinking

CD Contents

Foreword

Movie Time Social Learning

I learned about Anna Vagin's Movie Time Social Learning program at our first annual Social Thinking Providers Conference. During her engaging presentation, Anna outlined how mediating strategies used in the framework of movie watching can foster a student's ability to think socially: to read context; interpret thoughts, feelings, and plans; make predictions about social behavior; interpret emotional cues; and use narrative language to discuss social interactions.

Anna explained how her program increases students' awareness of the subtle rules underlying social communication by exploring relationships between the movie characters. She also shared the different lessons she developed to serve a range of developmental ages and levels of social functioning.

While I had used clips from movies and TV shows with my students for years to examine social behavior as I developed ideas in Social Thinking, I hadn't considered a more comprehensive curriculum to guide this type of teaching until I ran across Anna's inventive program. The many examples in this book make clear the breadth of learning that is possible with Movie Time Social Learning. This is a promising new teaching strategy for those working in the growing field of social cognitive treatments.

One of the greatest challenges in teaching social thinking — finding interesting, imaginative and enjoyable ways for students of all ages to study complex social situations — is something the Movie Time program addresses successfully. As Anna points out, movies allow us to study social interactions as they unfold across time. By hitting the pause button, we allow for deeper examination and discussion on topics of interest to many children — friendship, personal challenges, bullying, etc. By talking about how the characters (people) relate to each other, students develop their social understanding.

Social learning, which for most people is intuitive starting at birth, is arduous for anyone with social learning challenges. In teaching these students, we now are recognizing the need to shift from traditional methods that focus on specific social skills to more active strategies that explore the full depth of social engagement. Anna points out that it's not just the children who need to learn new ideas. Several chapters in *Movie Time Social Learning* present nonverbal, visual, and verbal mediating strategies that provide essential information for therapists, teachers, and parents who are supporting students who have social thinking challenges.

Students with social thinking challenges will be engaged in social learning throughout their childhood and into their adult years, so an important question is: How do we motivate our students to keep exploring and learning about the social process over time? Movie Time Social Learning joins other innovative programs that seek to answer this question, such as Carol Gray's Social Stories™; Kari Dunn Buron's Incredible 5-Point Scale; Tony Attwood's CAT-kit; and the Superflex Superhero Social Thinking curriculum developed by Stephanie Madrigal and me (2008).

The proverbial "a picture is worth a thousand words" is no more true than when exploring how movies can help to teach social learning. Movie Time Social Learning takes an engaging activity that many students already love and uses it as a jumping-off point to study the intricacies of social interaction as well as the depth and range of emotions we experience in our lives.

Movie Time Social Learning's dynamic format succeeds in tying together the strands of social thinking that so often challenge children with social cognitive limitations. The concepts Anna articulates so thoughtfully in this book will give professionals as well as parents a fresh and sophisticated way to teach social comprehension and social expression and to support students as they generalize the concepts to their own lives.

Michelle Garcia Winner
Founder of Social Thinking
San Jose, CA
November, 2012

Hit the pause button, hit the pause button!
Stop — I wanna tell you what they're thinking…

– Eli, 10, during a Movie Time Social Learning activity

Chapter 1

Introducing Movie Time Social Learning

Two children and I were watching a movie in which a frog landed on a diner's plate in a fancy restaurant. We viewed this scene several times using Movie Time Social Learning activities, talking about what the people at the table might have been thinking and feeling. Then a casual remark I made about a personal experience ignited an unexpected and lively discussion.

Anna (me): Well, I've never eaten a frog, but I did eat dried grasshoppers in Mexico once — they weren't bad…
Jonah: Yeah, I saw that on TV, dried bugs!
Justin: And in chocolate. My brother ate a lollipop with a scorpion. He got it at the Academy of Sciences. *He* liked it, but *I* thought it was gross! (*He showed his understanding of perspective, that their two opinions were different.*)
Jonah: What'd the grasshoppers taste like? Do you still have 'em?
Justin: (*shifting his gaze from Jonah to me*) Bring 'em in — I wanna see!
Jonah: Yeah, yeah, we wanna see 'em!

These two children had worked together in a therapy group at my office but rarely had expressed much interest in each other and had previously had only limited spontaneous conversations. This day, they left the session giggling together. The next time they came to my office, they started a joint campaign to get me to bring in my dried grasshoppers. A new social connection had been made!

The Power of Movies

From a young age, children with social learning differences may be accustomed to watching television and videos without noticing much about the interactions on the screen. Such viewing often is considered "downtime." Movie Time Social Learning uses the recreational appeal of movies to help children expand their social understanding. This therapeutic program of facilitated viewing and discussion of carefully selected children's movies, helps children with a range of social cognitive challenges explore and dissect social relationships, thoughts, and feelings in a therapy or classroom setting or at home.

A primary aspect of social interaction is the impermanence of interpersonal moments. Once a word is spoken, an expression passes across a face, or a gesture is made, it vanishes. We must notice and process the information immediately, or we move forward with incomplete or incorrect information. While there may be repeated cues or corrections, in life there are no pause, rewind, or replay buttons, as there are in Movie Time Social Learning.

Using this program, children gain the opportunity to view and replay onscreen interactions to practice thinking and talking about how people relate to each other. The therapist, teacher, or parent acts as the facilitator and freezes, slows, or replays specific scenes in a movie, taking advantage of the capabilities of today's DVD players and digital players to freeze a moment in social time. Children can unpack the moment and build their social thinking, perspective taking, and narrative language skills without time pressure. Through this practice, they increase their understanding of the social concepts that are crucial to social thought and are introduced to new vocabulary they can use to talk about their interactions with others. Success with Movie Time tasks builds skills and confidence in thinking socially that they can then apply to their own behavior.

Movie Time Social Learning uses the recreational appeal of movies to help children expand their social understanding.

Of course, there are other ways to make social moments last for review and discussion; Movie Time Social Learning is one option for the therapeutic toolbox. Video recording interactions and role-playing are certainly well documented, widely used therapeutic techniques that help children review and study their social behavior. However, an advantage of Movie Time is that it lets children discuss the social reasons behind overt social behavior without having to look directly at their own behavior and make careful observations of the many components that make up interactions.

Asking the Right Questions

Social thought involves making quick judgments based on the context. A monumental amount of information is available to us in our constantly changing environment. As we process it, our neurotypical social brain is expected to form questions to direct our thoughts.

- Questions about context: Where am I? Who else is here? What's happening here that will affect me? What are the social expectations in this context?
- Questions about perspective: What knowledge do I have? What knowledge do others around me have? What are others thinking about right now? What does that mean to me?
- Questions about feelings: How am I feeling? How are others feeling? How intense are these feelings? How do these emotional states change, and can I predict their direction? How will I react to moderate shifts in my feelings and the feelings of others?
- Questions about nonverbal information: What is each person's face and body saying? Does it match their spoken words, or do I have to make sense of a discrepancy? What am I supposed to do about that information?
- Questions about conversation: What are people talking about? How are they expressing their opinions? Do they mean the words they're saying, or are mixed or indirect messages being communicated? What can I add to the conversation that will be relevant and interesting?
- Questions about cause and effect: What are the possible consequences of events or actions (including my own)? What kind of influence does context have on me and on the people around me? How can I tailor my reactions to those social consequences, making appropriate changes to my behavior?

Our answers guide most of us through our lives, directing our related social behaviors (social skills) with relative success. But what happens for those whose brains don't form these questions? Given the complex list of necessary social judgments and decisions, it isn't surprising that in "real time," students with social learning challenges are overwhelmed. Movie Time Social Learning can increase a child's self-confidence in understanding social interactions, while decreasing social passivity and/or anxiety.

Relevant Themes and Complex Characters

Many children's movies, based on familiar stories, portray recurrent themes relevant to their lives — finding and keeping relationships, overcoming obstacles, recovering from loss, and valuing internal characteristics over outer appearances. Movies often present the course of intimate relationships over time. Characters often show themselves to be more than they initially appear. Our early judgments may prove to be incorrect and shortsighted. As in life, it's only when we become familiar with someone that we appreciate the person's true value.

- Inspector Clouseau (*The Pink Panther*) isn't totally inept; ultimately he solves the case and triumphs — humorously — over the scheming chief inspector.
- The memory-impaired Dory (*Finding Nemo*) provides Nemo with helpful information at critical moments.
- While what we notice first about Hermione Granger (*Harry Potter* series) is her caustic wit and exceptional brain, over time we appreciate her sense of humor and empathy.

As we watch a movie, we develop relationships with the characters as they themselves form bonds with each other and observe their failures or successes in a fictional social world. We are witness to "relationship moments" — those scenes in which some telling, intimate change occurs within or between characters.

Through movies, we can explore with students what makes connections between people work (or not work). We can break down life experiences into many elements — thoughts, actions, and feelings — that occur in a wider range of contexts than we're often able to find in our day-to-day lives. Students become comfortable with the ideas and vocabulary involved in social thought, which they then can apply to their own behavior. Success with Movie Time tasks builds skills and confidence in thinking socially.

A Variety of Relationships

When working with Movie Time Social Learning, students experience multiple possibilities for relationships: one with the movie itself, another with the mediating adult, and a third with peers. In the first relationship, students become involved with the characters and events of the story, though they're not involved in any direct interaction. A primary goal is to encourage students to be active, engaged observers who are thinking about what's happening onscreen. Rather than having them be passive viewers, we encourage students to really think about the movie they're watching and relate it to their own life experiences.

Each student is also in an active social relationship with the adult facilitator, whether it be a therapist, teacher, other professional, or parent. As we ask probing questions and suggest directions of thought while doing Movie Time tasks, we enable students to delve more deeply into a movie than when they watch without intervention. When working through movie scenes, students practice key social thinking skills and interact with you, the adult, in the following ways:

- Discussing a shared reference (the movie)
- Shifting from joint focus on the screen to focus on each other
- Reasoning and solving problems together
- Clarifying ideas and opinions
- Following logical questioning
- Probing complicated events
- Sharing feeling states

In Movie Time Social Learning, this adult is also called a "mediator" and the strategies used "mediating strategies." See Chapter 3 for details about the role of the Movie Time Social Learning mediator and Chapters 4, 5, and 6 for information about suggested mediating strategies.

A Time of Engagement

Finally, most children enjoy movies, particularly when they know the films have been chosen specifically for them. As they watch, even in a structured, therapeutic setting (or perhaps because of it), they usually become more animated, spontaneous, and engaged. As they figure out more details about the characters, setting, and plot, everything makes more sense and watching becomes even more fun. If the students are viewing the movies in a group (or at home with siblings), discussions often prompt conversations between children, as in the example of the dried grasshoppers at the beginning of this chapter. This gives students a wonderful chance to talk and listen to each other.

Foundation in Social Cognition

The Movie Time Social Learning program has its foundation in social cognition and utilizes many of the Social Thinking concepts developed by speech language pathologist Michelle Garcia Winner, which encompass "the interpretation of all social behavior and tasks that require social interpretation" (Winner, 2008). For most of us, social thinking is something intuitive; we naturally make observations about where we are, as well as the thoughts, feelings, and plans of the people we are with. We pick up on direct and indirect information others are sending, and modify our behavior based on that information. As we move through our lives, we're almost constantly engaged in social thinking. We take for granted what's actually a pretty complicated set of cognitive processes.

To understand the expectations of a situation, we must evaluate the context, sorting a mass of information from multiple channels. Such thought requires perspective taking, or the understanding that each individual has thoughts, experiences and opinions that are different from our own (Baron-Cohen, 1995; Wolfberg, 1999; Winner, 2008). To think in someone else's shoes, we need to evaluate what information that person is privy to and figure out how it fits with what we know about the world.

Through her work, Winner has codified a vocabulary as part of her Social Thinking methodology and materials, making it easier to work with the core concepts (Winner, 2005, 2008). Phrases including "thinking with your eyes," "making a smart guess," "social smarts" and "expected/unexpected behavior" (Winner & Crooke, 2008) have offered professionals working in the field of social cognition simple yet precise ways to encapsulate the ideas behind social thought.

Movie Time Social Learning helps to link the components of Social Thinking in a structured but dynamic learning process, supporting children in:

- Identifying contextual and fundamental "thinking with your eyes" information
- Discerning feeling states
- Expanding emotional vocabulary
- Understanding and tracking multiple perspectives
- Interpreting tone, indirectness, and facial, nonverbal, and gestural information
- Discussing expected and unexpected behaviors and consequences
- Experiencing empathy with characters

Note: The activities in this book assume that those who use Movie Time Social Learning with students are already familiar with Winner's Social Thinking concepts, vocabulary terms, and teaching framework. To review these concepts in more depth, it's recommended you refer to the Social Thinking books listed in the "References section of Appendix C" and visit www.socialthinking.com.

My Path to Movie Time Social Learning

I've always worked in the social cognition field, beginning with a focus on the importance of pragmatics — the social use of language. In the late 1970s, when I was an undergraduate at the University of California, Santa Barbara, pragmatics was the hot theory in speech and language pathology. It placed everything that was known about speech and language development within context. I was fortunate to have Carol Prutting, one of the foremost thinkers and scholars in the area of clinical pragmatics, as one of my undergraduate professors. With pragmatics, correctness or incorrectness of communication was evaluated from a "well, it depends..." point of view, recognizing that rules about communication weren't carved in stone. Prutting's passion and creativity in exploring how the pragmatics of disordered language could be described and measured (Prutting & Kirchner, 1987) led her enthusiastic students as well as her peers, to question what defined "communicative competence," a new term coined during that era to describe how well people are able to use their verbal and nonverbal language skills (Schiefelbusch, 1984).

Pragmatics was just the beginning of examining communication in new ways. Emerging fields such as social cognition have provided more ideas about the social brain. The past 30 years have seen explosive growth in the field of language pathology, as the traditional divisions — phonology, morphology, semantics, and syntax — have expanded to include overriding language use, executive function (how we organize and manage information), and social thought.

For many years, my work focused on the early development of interpersonal, affective connection. As I began working with more and more students on the autism spectrum in the mid-1980s, I looked for materials to support their visual processing preferences, with particular interest in providing them with social information based in movement rather than in static pictures. As I experimented with movies, I found myself following a consistent format of questioning and visual supports, which I began to store and re-use, consistently impressed with how much students enjoyed movie work — there was Movie Time!

Breaking Down Social Thought

Across the program, students are guided through a progressive series of tasks, from the simpler job of figuring out what characters are thinking, feeling, and planning, to more complex explorations of how relationships develop and students' own empathic reactions.

A variety of children's movies are appropriate for Movie Time Social Learning. It's recommended that you start with the titles for which lesson plans are provided on the CD that accompanies this book. There are lesson plans for seven movies to use for different age groups and levels of social thinking. The lesson plans include information about stopping points, questions to ask, and other suggestions and cautions. See Chapter 2 for more information about each of these movies. Chapter 2 also suggests other recommended movies and tips for selecting additional movies of your own.

The techniques and mediating strategies presented in this book are applicable to any work in social cognition. Movie Time Social Learning was developed to be one tool on a shelf full of materials. Generalization is an important component of social learning, so once a student has worked hard identifying emotions in movie scenes, give them the opportunity to identify similar emotions in other therapy situations, on the playground at school, or the waiting room at your office. Remember to constantly bring learned skills into new situations.

Students from Preschool to High School

Movie Time Social Learning can be used with students with social cognitive challenges from preschool to high school age who:

- Have verbal language with an MLU (mean length of utterance) of 3.0 morphemes or higher. For MTSL use at home, can speak in short phrases and have some experience watching movies or television, either alone or with family.
- Can follow simple directions
- Can maintain joint attention for ten minutes in an engaging activity
- Can maintain a well-regulated state (given sufficient supports) for ten minutes
- Have begun work with identification of emotions in themselves and others
- Are familiar with the foundation concepts of social thinking — that people have thoughts and we can try to figure them out

I've used Movie Time activities with all ages in one-on-one work as well as with small groups of up to four students. Working with a child individually allows you to really tailor your pace and overall work to that student's specific needs and can be a wonderful format even when working with students with more advanced skills. A group format allows for peer interaction and social group experience. Which format you select will, very likely, depend on where you work, your caseload, and your schedule! If possible, experiment with both and find what works best for you and the students with whom you work. It's a good idea to start with one or two students at a time as you begin to use the techniques. As you gain experience, you can set up larger groups, although groups larger than four students aren't recommended.

You can use Movie Time Social Learning as part of an ongoing Social Thinking therapy program once or twice a week as you work through a movie, and then take a break before starting another film. If you decide to use Movie Time Social Learning as an after-school (club type) offering or a summer social camp, just make sure all the participants have a level of overall ability and social knowledge (see above) to make your efforts successful. Movie Time is also a great program to send home to parents!

The Movie Time format accommodates a variety of social learning challenges and skill levels. Of course, Movie Time Social Learning isn't for everyone. The program probably wouldn't be appropriate for children with significant cognitive impairment, extreme language learning challenges, a high level of sensory integration impairment, or a minimal awareness of others. These children work better with interventions that target functional communication.

Mindreader Categories

At the start of the Movie Time Social Learning program, you place students in one of three categories of social learners, called Mindreaders, discussed in more detail in "Student Mindreader Levels" in Chapter 2. In general, Junior Mindreaders are learning to identify and label the thoughts, feelings, and plans of others; Moving Up Mindreaders require support to work with multiple perspectives and a broader range of feelings; and Varsity Mindreaders are building a more sophisticated feeling vocabulary and learning how complicated interpersonal events influence relationships. The specific movies students watch differ depending on their Mindreader group and are based on what's developmentally appropriate for that group of social thinker. Movies vary according to the amount of information, the speed at which it's presented, the complexity of the story line, and the intensity of relationships depicted.

Social Thinking Tasks

No matter which movie they view or which Mindreader group they're in, students participate in three different types of Social Thinking activities as they watch the movie. Each of these tasks addresses skills that are necessary in successful social interactions:

- Spy Eye: Students think with their eyes to explore context and what each character is doing, thinking, and feeling within that context.
- Detective Head: These activities involve perspective taking and promote the understanding of more complex social relationships and social subtleties, such as indirectness and politeness.
- Me Too!: These tasks focus on students making connections between characters and themselves to explore the foundations of empathy.

Spy Eye tasks feature the easiest activities (though still valuable for Varsity Mindreaders), followed by Detective Head and Me Too! Where you begin and the goals you set for particular students depend on their Movie Time Social Learning category placement. You can repeat the same movie with the same child or group of children. Repeat viewings can be used to review tasks for greater understanding or to try different tasks.

The tasks in Movie Time Social Learning groups are not strictly linear; frequently you'll find yourself working on more than one type of task at the same time during a discussion of a movie scene. You may find yourself discussing how a character feels (a Spy Eye task) as well as encouraging students to remember times when they've had similar experiences (a Me Too! task). In other words, you don't have to complete all of the Spy Eye tasks before moving on to Detective Head or Me Too! activities. With practice, you'll be able to gauge how much discussion about a scene will benefit a child or group. You'll stop the movies frequently for review. Though the tasks are presented in short segments, you might easily spend 20 or 30 minutes on each scene.

Coming Up

In the following chapters, you'll learn how to use Movie Time Social Learning with students.

- **Chapter 2** Getting Ready — designating Mindreader categories for each student; gathering movies, supplies, and equipment; and communicating with administrators and families about the program
- **Chapter 3** Places Everyone! Your Role as Mediator — working with a movie audience of students, including suggestions for helping students regulate before they watch, strategies for sessions, and when to take a break
- **Chapter 4** Quiet on the Set! Silence and Other Nonverbal Mediating Strategies — body-based, nonverbal mediation strategies (silence, listening to intonation, pacing, gestures, and facial expressions) that you can use with Movie Time Social Learning
- **Chapter 5** Mark Up Those Cue Cards! Knowing How to Help Visually — visual tools, such as emotions strips and feeling lists, thought bubbles, and text-based organizers, that can support student work
- **Chapter 6** Dialogue Coaches at the Ready! Knowing How to Help with Words — verbal mediating strategies for use with Movie Time Social Learning, such as intonation, open-ended questions, verbal cues, conjunctions, restating, and expressing uncertainty
- **Chapter 7** First Lessons: Spy Eye Tasks — exploring context and the feelings, thoughts, and plans of movie characters
- **Chapter 8** More Complex Thought: Detective Head Tasks — more complex activities that involve perspective taking and multiple characters
- **Chapter 9** Practicing Empathy: Me Too! Tasks — activities that explore students' empathy with movie characters
- **Chapter 10** Off and Running: Generalizing What Students Have Learned — suggestions for applying knowledge learned to other contexts, including at home
- **Appendix A** Visual Aids — templates to photocopy and use with Movie Time Social Learning (also provided on the CD)
- **Appendix B** Letters and Forms — for use with families, administrators, and staff (also provided on the CD)
- **Appendix C** Resources and References — movies list, other resources, and references

Included on the CD that accompanies this book are seven detailed lesson plans for movies intended for different levels of Mindreaders as well as templates, handouts, and letters that you can use with the program.

With Movie Time Social Learning, building social understanding is fun. Greater understanding, in turn, leads to greater enjoyment of the movie's story as well as expanding confidence that the social world is not so mysterious.

I read in a book once that having a child with special needs is like getting on an airplane for a trip. You think you are going to Venice, but then the stewardess tells you you have landed in Holland. Well, you can spend your time crying for the gondolas, or you can get out and enjoy the windmills. It's not quite what you had expected, but it is beautiful all the same.

—**Anna Perera,** in *The Elephant in the Playroom*

Chapter 2

Getting Ready

Movie Time Social Learning offers novel, exciting tools for teachers and therapists to use when teaching social thinking skills. As with any new program, however, it's important to be thoughtful before diving in. Movie Time Social Learning is most effective with ample preparation. This chapter will help you get started.

As you prepare to use the program, consider these questions about the student, the chosen movie, technical issues, and communicating with administrators and parents:

- What's the appropriate Mindreader designation for this student: Junior, Moving Up, or Varsity Mindreader? (See the next section, "Student Mindreader Levels.")
- What are this student's previous experiences watching movies? Which activities and which movies are most appropriate for this child? (See Chapters 7, 8, and 9 for details about each type of activity: Spy Eye, Detective Head, and Me Too!)
- Which movies will I use with each student or group of students? Why did I make these choices? (See "Choosing the Movies" in this chapter.)
- Am I familiar with the movie I'm showing? Do I know which parts I do and don't want to show? Do I know what my goals are and which scenes will address them? (See the lesson plans on the CD.)
- Do I have the equipment I need and have it set up so it will work? Have I practiced with it, especially the pause and rewind buttons? (See "DVD Players and Furnishings" in this chapter.)

- What will help this child maintain a regulated state for successful movie viewing? Do I have these materials at hand? (See "Regulatory Aids" in this chapter.)
- Have I communicated with administrators about the program and set up how I'll monitor progress toward goals? (See "Introducing the Program to Administrators, Staff, and Families" in this chapter.)
- Have I explained Movie Time Social Learning to the student's parent(s) and obtained appropriate releases? Are there any media restrictions in this family? (See "Obtaining Parental Releases" in this chapter.)

Student Mindreader Levels

One of the first steps in beginning Movie Time Social Learning is determining which Mindreader level is the best fit for each student. You'll use your personal observations of the characteristics of the three types of Mindreaders (as summarized in Figure 2.1) to determine whether the student you're working with is a Junior, Moving Up, or Varsity Mindreader. You begin by considering what you know about each student's level of language ability and overall narrative skills; perspective taking ability; and abilities to understand, identify, and use the vocabulary of emotions.

The Mindreader groups are general categories only. If you start the program and feel a student might actually fit better in a different category, simply make the switch. It may take a while to develop your placement skills as these are tricky judgments to make.

	Junior Mindreaders	Moving Up Mindreaders	Varsity Mindreaders
Language	• Usually have language delay • Have no functional use of conjunctions • Have a very hard time telling a story; poor narrative skills	• Often have language delay • Demonstrate emerging but infrequent use of conjunctions • Tell very basic stories, sometimes with no clear sequence; limited narrative skills	• May or may not have language delay • Use some basic conjunctions (e.g., "but," "because") • Can describe events, but with limited details and few emotional or relational connections

	Junior Mindreaders	Moving Up Mindreaders	Varsity Mindreaders
Perspective Taking	• With high support are beginning to recognize that thoughts, feelings, and plans of others can be different from their own	• With moderate support can identify others' perspectives, but require a lot of processing time; with high support can work to understand and keep multiple perspectives in mind	• With support can identify contrasting perspectives and make predictions about behavior, but often still make mistakes or disregard information when considering their own actions
Understanding of Emotions	• Have difficulty identifying emotions in themselves and others • Are beginning to use labels such as happy, sad, and angry • Require high support to consider reasons behind emotions	• Require significant processing time to identify emotions in most situations • Identify happy, sad, angry with relative accuracy, but have difficulty with gradations of emotions • Struggle to explain the reasons behind emotions	• Demonstrate emerging ability to read emotions of others in real time • Are learning how to code emotions accurately in real time and are learning more complicated emotional terms (e.g., annoyed, frustrated, depressed, explosive) • Demonstrate emerging ability to explain the reasons behind emotions

	Junior Mindreaders	Moving Up Mindreaders	Varsity Mindreaders
Social Thinking–Social Communication Profile™ (ST-SCP) Category (Winner, Crooke, and Madrigal, 2011) (See www.social thinking. com for profile information.)	Generally Junior Mindreaders are in the Challenged Social Communicator (CSC) category.	Generally many Moving Up Mindreaders are in the Emerging Social Communicator (ESC) category.	Generally Varsity Mindreaders are in the Nuance Challenged Social Communicator (NCSC) category, which includes the Weak Interactive Social Communicator (WISC) and the Socially Anxious Social Communicator (SASC) subcategories.

Figure 2.1. Criteria for placing students into one of the three categories

Language Skills

Language ability affects how students understand and are able to talk about what's happening. When considering this key area, examine:

- Does this child have a diagnosed language delay?
- Can this child use complex sentences, or does her language consist of simple sentences? Is she using any conjunctions in her spontaneous language?
- How does this student tell a story — does he struggle in the retelling? Is it unclear how and why the events unfolded? Can you understand the sequence the student has relayed, or are you totally confused?

Perspective Taking

Next, you'll consider a primary determinant of social effectiveness: perspective taking ability, the capacity to understand that others around us may have thoughts, feelings, and plans that may be different from our own. Our perspective taking skills help us determine how much information to give to the person with whom we're interacting — to figure out what that person already knows. Finally, when we're talking to someone, our perspective taking abilities guide us in understanding what the person may be thinking about us, so we can make corrections as needed (Baron-Cohen, 1995; Winner, 2000).

Perspective taking is a particularly difficult skill for children with social learning challenges. As part of her in-depth work developing current ideas about Social Thinking, Michelle Garcia Winner has written and spoken extensively about the perspective taking abilities of individuals with social cognitive challenges. The Social Thinking–Social Communication Profile™, a scale Winner created with colleagues Pamela Crooke and

Stephanie Madrigal (2011), considers a number of factors in determining overall social communication success:

- Understanding our own and others' thoughts and emotions (perspective taking)
- Emotional coping
- Peer interactions
- Self-awareness
- Social problem-solving
- Academic skills
- Bullying and manipulation

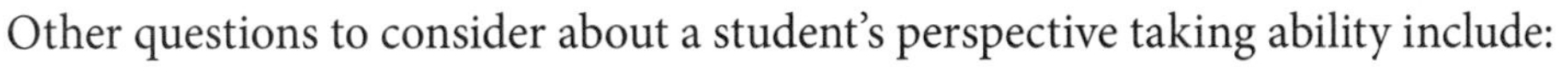

Other questions to consider about a student's perspective taking ability include:

- Does this student recognize that others may have thoughts and feelings that are different from his own? Students who have difficulties with this are likely Junior Mindreaders.
- How much time and support does the student require to differentiate among multiple perspectives? If a lot of time is spent helping students discover hidden rules and others' thoughts, the students are likely Junior Mindreaders.
- Can the student keep multiple perspectives in her working memory at the same time, or does she become easily confused when considering these differing thoughts? If students can discuss others' perspectives, even if they seem to be very self-centered in their own behavior, they're probably Moving Up Mindreaders.
- Is the student able to discuss multiple perspectives in therapy yet makes many errors in judging the perspectives of others in the outside world? Though the child doesn't necessarily stand out in a crowd, he still has significant difficulties getting along with peers and developing friendships. These children are probably Varsity Mindreaders.

Understanding Emotions

Related to students' perspective taking ability is the degree to which they're comfortable and accurate when discussing and recognizing their own and others' feelings. When thinking about a child's ability to understand and talk about emotions, consider:

- Can he easily identify and accurately label feelings in himself?
- Can she easily identify and accurately label the feelings of others?
- Does his emotional vocabulary limit him to using only adjectives such as sad, angry, and happy?
- Can she judge the strength of a feeling, differentiating a "little bit angry" from "really angry"?

- Is he able to explain the reasons behind the feelings of others, or does he bog down in figuring out *why* people feel the way they do?
- Does she understand that people have emotional reactions in response to her behavior?

If you're uncertain about which category to choose, err on the conservative side.

It's always easier to challenge children who turn out to be more adept than you initially thought than to simplify tasks for children who struggle with tasks beyond their abilities. Being able to feel successful with Movie Time Social Learning results in feelings of competence and improves the likelihood that children will take more risks as they move through increasingly challenging tasks.

Choosing the Movies

There I was, watching Shrek *in therapy with two children. All of a sudden … wait a minute … did Shrek really say "ass"?! And with such expression and emphasis! These children sure noticed it. Gee, I never noticed when I watched the movie at home. What if these children go home and tell what new vocabulary they learned in speech today? Help!*

One crucial decision is picking an appropriate movie for your students. There's no perfect movie, at least none that I've found. I've developed my list of recommended movies from a number of sources. Although you can purchase these movies, you can also depend on local libraries, video rental stores, Netflix, and other sources. Some can even be viewed on YouTube. All of the movies referred to in this book are usually easy to find: all were released between 2000 and 2009.

Note that the more commercial movies, even those referred to in this book, tend to reflect popular culture, including its unsavory aspects. Be judicious in what you show; it's fine to be overly cautious in this regard. The lesson plans available on the CD include tips for specific scenes you might want to skip for these reasons.

Always check the rating level of movies that you use. Initially I was surprised that *Shrek* is rated PG, not G. *Never show an R-rated movie.* Make sure to give information to parents about the ratings of movies you'll show and have them sign a release form. Sample parent letters and releases are in Appendix B.

The CD includes lesson plans for the seven recommended movies described in the next sections (movie lengths provided are approximate). Each lesson plan identifies segments or scenes to discuss and provides suggestions for Spy Eye, Detective Head, and Me Too! activities for each segment, including questions you can pose, helpful visual tools to address specific tasks, and other tips and alerts. Scenes that are most valuable to cover for Moving Up and Varsity Mindreaders are noted with a star ☆.

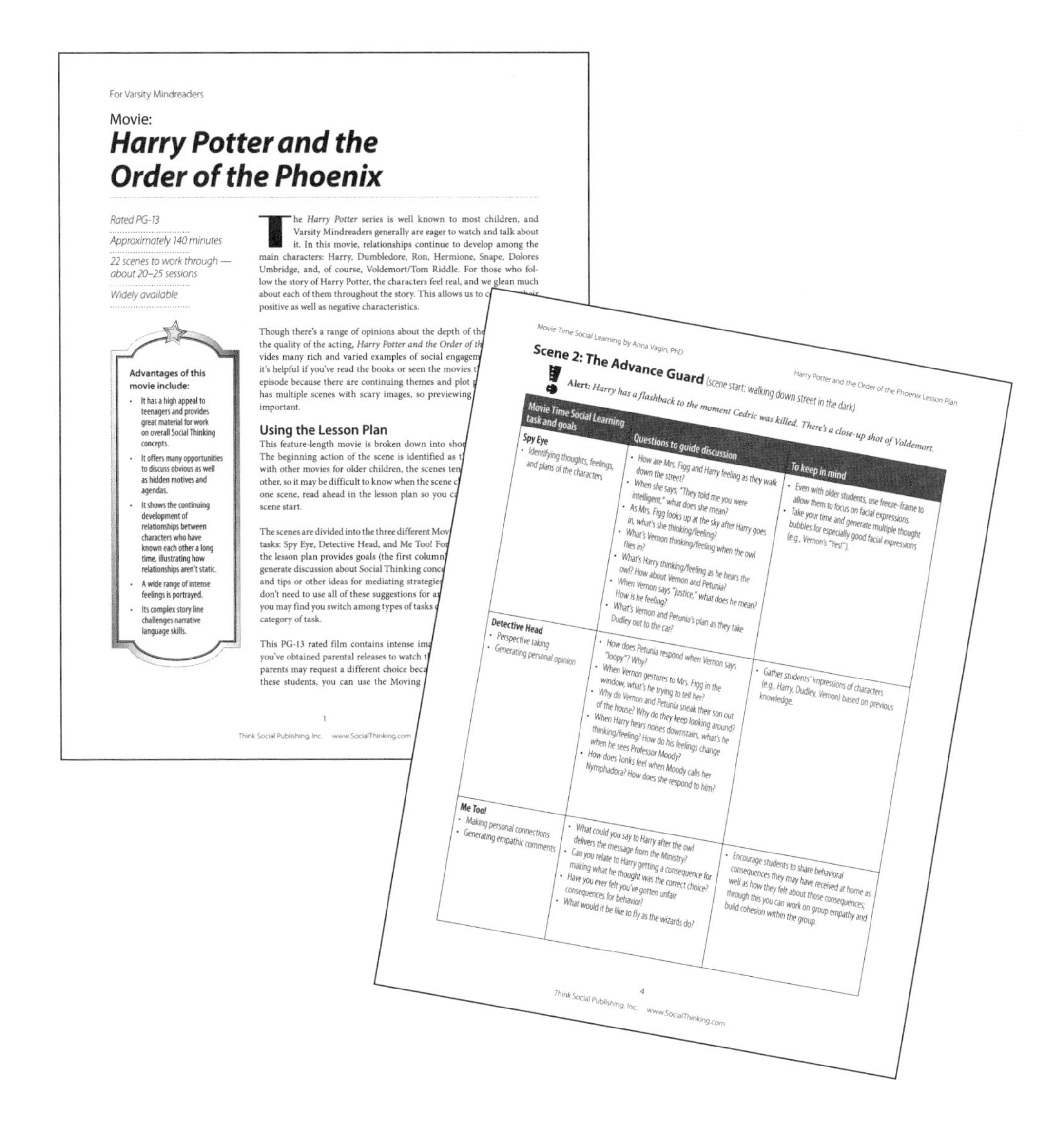

For Varsity Mindreaders

Movie:

Harry Potter and the Order of the Phoenix

Rated PG-13

Approximately 140 minutes

22 scenes to work through — about 20–25 sessions

Widely available

Advantages of this movie include:

- It has a high appeal to teenagers and provides great material for work on overall Social Thinking concepts.
- It offers many opportunities to discuss obvious as well as hidden motives and agendas.
- It shows the continuing development of relationships between characters who have known each other a long time, illustrating how relationships aren't static.
- A wide range of intense feelings is portrayed.
- Its complex story line challenges narrative language skills.

The *Harry Potter* series is well known to most children, and Varsity Mindreaders generally are eager to watch and talk about it. In this movie, relationships continue to develop among the main characters: Harry, Dumbledore, Ron, Hermione, Snape, Dolores Umbridge, and, of course, Voldemort/Tom Riddle. For those who follow the story of Harry Potter, the characters feel real, and we glean much about each of them throughout the story. This allows us to c… positive as well as negative characteristics.

Though there's a range of opinions about the depth of the… the quality of the acting, *Harry Potter and the Order of th…* vides many rich and varied examples of social engagem… it's helpful if you've read the books or seen the movies t… episode because there are continuing themes and plot … has multiple scenes with scary images, so previewing … important.

Using the Lesson Plan

This feature-length movie is broken down into sho… The beginning action of the scene is identified as t… with other movies for older children, the scenes ten… other, so it may be difficult to know when the scene c… one scene, read ahead in the lesson plan so you ca… scene start.

The scenes are divided into the three different Mov… tasks: Spy Eye, Detective Head, and Me Too! Fo… the lesson plan provides goals (the first column)… generate discussion about Social Thinking conc… and tips or other ideas for mediating strategie… don't need to use all of these suggestions for a… you may find you switch among types of tasks … category of task.

This PG-13 rated film contains intense ima… you've obtained parental releases to watch t… parents may request a different choice beca… these students, you can use the Moving …

1

Think Social Publishing, Inc. www.SocialThinking.com

Movie Time Social Learning by Anna Vagin, PhD

Harry Potter and the Order of the Phoenix Lesson Plan

Scene 2: The Advance Guard (scene start: walking down street in the dark)

Alert: *Harry has a flashback to the moment Cedric was killed. There's a close-up shot of Voldemort.*

Movie Time Social Learning task and goals	Questions to guide discussion	To keep in mind
Spy Eye • Identifying thoughts, feelings, and plans of the characters	• How are Mrs. Figg and Harry feeling as they walk down the street? • When she says, "They told me you were intelligent," what does she mean? • As Mrs. Figg looks up at the sky after Harry goes in, what's she thinking/feeling? • What's Vernon thinking/feeling when the owl flies in? • What's Harry thinking/feeling as he hears the owl? How about Vernon and Petunia? • When Vernon says "justice," what does he mean? How is he feeling? • What's Vernon and Petunia's plan as they take Dudley out to the car?	• Even with older students, use freeze-frame to allow them to focus on facial expressions. • Take your time and generate multiple thought bubbles for especially good facial expressions (e.g., Vernon's "Yes!").
Detective Head • Perspective taking • Generating personal opinion	• How does Petunia respond when Vernon says "loopy"? Why? • When Vernon gestures to Mrs. Figg in the window, what's he trying to tell her? • Why do Vernon and Petunia sneak their son out of the house? Why do they keep looking around? • When Harry hears noises downstairs, what's he thinking/feeling? How do his feelings change when he sees Professor Moody? • How does Tonks feel when Moody calls her Nymphadora? How does she respond to him?	• Gather students' impressions of characters (e.g., Harry, Dudley, Vernon) based on previous knowledge.
Me Too! • Making personal connections • Generating empathic comments	• What could you say to Harry after the owl delivers the message from the Ministry? • Can you relate to Harry getting a consequence for making what he thought was the correct choice? • Have you ever felt you've gotten unfair consequences for behavior? • What would it be like to fly as the wizards do?	• Encourage students to share behavioral consequences they may have received at home as well as how they felt about those consequences; through this you can work on group empathy and build cohesion within the group.

4

Think Social Publishing, Inc. www.SocialThinking.com

For Junior Mindreaders

Knuffle Bunny (Scholastic Video Treasures)

- No rating
- 7 minutes long. It has three sections to work through, which will probably take one session of 30–40 minutes.
- Available from libraries or as a rental on a DVD with other short children's movies

This animated movie is based on illustrations from the book by the same name. Trixie and her dad, who live in Manhattan, go to the laundromat. Trixie takes along her beloved Knuffle Bunny that accidentally ends up in the wash. This is a good choice for Junior Mindreaders because it shows a wonderful range of feelings and several great examples of differing perspectives.

Whistle for Willie (Scholastic Video Collection)

- No rating
- 4 1/2 minutes long. It has two sections to work through, which will take one session of about 20 minutes.
- Available from libraries or as a rental on a disc with other short children's movies

This animated movie is based on illustrations from the book by the same name. A boy, Peter, wants to learn to whistle so he can call his dog, Willie. He tries and tries and is finally successful. To deal with his frustration while learning, he spins and draws. This movie is a good one because it portrays a story about sensory regulation and many other important social cognitive concepts, its visual simplicity, and its challenging perspective aspect (a boy hiding in a box) that students can easily reenact.

No Roses for Harry (Scholastic Video Collection)

- No rating
- 10 minutes long. It has four sections to work through, which will usually take two sessions, each about 20 minutes.
- Available at libraries, as a rental on a disc with other short children's movies

In this movie (based on the book of the same name), Harry, a family pet, receives an unwelcome gift and problem-solves around what to do with it. The conclusion is unexpected (unless you've read the book) and provides a funny twist that pleases the viewers. With a somewhat more complicated story line than *Knuffle Bunny*, this movie has clear pictures with great facial expressions and shows contrasting perspectives and portrayal of changes in characters' feeling states.

Frog Goes to Dinner (Scholastic Video Collection)

- No rating
- 12 minutes long. It has ten sections to work through, which will take three to five sessions, each about 20–30 minutes in length.
- Available at libraries or as a rental on a disc with other short children's movies

Frog Goes to Dinner puts Mercer Mayer's book of the same name on the movie screen. This movie with live actors follows the frog's adventures as he meanders through Le Grand Restaurant, causing havoc wherever he goes. The only audio is background music. This movie offers much material for exploring thoughts, feelings, and plans, and perspective taking.

For all children six years and younger as well as older children with limited or no practice with perspective taking, I use these four movies in the order presented. I recommend skipping *Knuffle Bunny* with children older than six who are familiar with the concept of reading minds and start with *Whistle for Willie.* Once Junior Mindreaders have completed *Whistle for Willie*, they could either watch *No Roses for Harry* if they need more practice with mindreading skills, or skip ahead to *Frog Goes to Dinner* if they seem ready for a live-action movie with more scenes and slightly more challenging material. Of course, you can always back up and watch movies you've skipped.

For Moving Up Mindreaders

Like Mike (Twentieth Century Fox Film Corporation)

- PG rating
- 96 minutes long. The movie has 22 scenes to work through, which will take about 10 or 12 sessions.
- Available at libraries and as a movie rental

A boy named Calvin, who is an orphan, gets some basketball shoes he thinks are magical, quickly propelling him onto a professional NBA team. The movie follows the sometimes bumpy relationship he develops with one of the players on the team who ends up adopting Calvin. Other story lines in the movie show relationships between kids and adults as well as kids working out various conflicts, demonstrating how it sometimes takes a while to work things out between people. This wonderful light-hearted movie offers a great and realistic message about friendship. Most older elementary and middle school students haven't seen it but love it. Even high school students find it appealing. Students' engagement makes it easy to work on challenging social cognitive concepts of perspective taking and development of relationships. See the lesson plan on the CD for more general information about using the movie.

The Indian in the Cupboard (Columbia Tri-Star Home Entertainment)

- PG rating
- 100 minutes long. It has 25 scenes to work through, which will take about 12 to 15 sessions.
- Available at libraries and as a movie rental

This is a great and engaging movie for older elementary and middle school students that carefully explores feelings within relationships between male characters. A young boy, Omri, is given a magical cabinet that brings to life a plastic American Indian figure named Little Bear. Omri and Little Bear come to grips with their unusual relationship and form an amazing friendship. Patrick, Omri's friend, is let in on the secret, which causes some conflict between the boys. The action gets pretty exciting, and its excellent script and acting make it a good one to work on empathic reactions. It also takes students through some intense subject matter (e.g., death, control over the lives of others, parental deceit) in a child-friendly way. Even though it includes some great action, this is a slower-paced movie that doesn't have a lot of scene shifts or quick dialogue. It provides rich material for Social Thinking work.

For Varsity Mindreaders

Harry Potter and the Order of the Phoenix (Warner Home Video)

- PG-13 rating
- 2 hours, 20 minutes long. It has 22 scenes to work through, and takes about 20 to 25 sessions, depending on the level of detailed discussion that's generated.
- Widely available

This very popular movie with a high appeal to teens is the fifth in the Harry Potter series. Although most students have seen it, they always seem willing to watch it again. As in all the Harry Potter movies, the theme of good versus evil is a bit cloudy — while some characters are easily identifiable as one or the other, the true motives behind the behavior of others are less clear. It offers many opportunities to discuss obvious as well as hidden motives and agendas and the nuances and subleties of behavior and language. It portrays the continuing development of relationships between characters who have known each other a long time, and characters show a wide range of intense feelings. It provides great material for work on overall Social Thinking concepts.

Note that this movie contains intense images. A few parents may request a different choice because of this film's content. For these students, you can use the Moving Up Mindreader movies; there will still be much to discuss.

Other Recommended Movies

The following are several additional movies you might want to use when you're ready to develop your own lesson plans for students. I've used all of them with students. You'll see many of them referred to in examples included in this book:

- *Finding Nemo*, rated G (Walt Disney Studios Home Entertainment), Junior and Moving Up Mindreader levels
- *The Pink Panther*, rated PG (Sony Pictures Home Entertainment), Moving Up and Varsity Mindreader levels
- *Pooh's Grand Adventure: The Search for Christopher Robin*, rated G (Buena Vista Home Entertainment), for Junior Mindreader level
- *The Red Balloon*, rated G (Janus Films), Junior and Moving Up Mindreader levels
- *Sylvester and the Magic Pebble*, no rating (Scholastic Video Collection), Junior and Moving Up Mindreader levels
- *Fly Away Home*, rated PG (Sony Pictures Home Entertainment), for Moving Up Mindreader level
- *Akeelah and the Bee*, rated PG (Lions Gate Films), for Moving Up Mindreader level
- *Shrek*, rated PG (DreamWorks Home Entertainment), Moving Up and Varsity Mindreader levels
- *Confessions of a Teenage Drama Queen*, rated PG (Walt Disney Pictures), Varsity Mindreader level

Selecting Other Movies

As you preview possible other movies to use with Movie Time Social Learning, consider these factors:

- Make sure there are some "good relationships" to track — those in which relationships develop or change over time.
- Look for multiple instances where problems develop and are solved. That's where you'll be able to work on narrative language and track multiple perspectives.
- Limit the amount of action without meaningful dialogue; not too many musical numbers or quick action (battle) filler, unless you plan to skip those.
- Be mindful of ratings, questionable language, and scary elements, even for older students.
- For beginning Junior Mindreaders, you may want to find movies based on familiar books or characters.
- Movies that use still frames based on a book's illustrations and animated movies work well with Junior Mindreaders; look at live action ones for Moving Up and Varsity Mindreaders.

- Movies for Moving Up Mindreaders have more rapidly developing scenes, more complex relationships, include more nuances, and more mature themes than those for Junior Mindreaders.
- Consider pacing — children who need more time to process will do best with movies that move at a slower pace and have fewer jumps between scenes.

Gathering Equipment and Other Materials

DVD Players and Furnishings

When you play a movie in a therapeutic setting, a TV, large monitor, or a computer screen (15 to 17 inches works well) is optimal. A small DVD player can suffice, especially with only one or two students. (You can also play movies on a tablet device that's connected to a TV monitor.) You'll be moving among the pause, rewind, and play buttons frequently, freezing scenes in which the most visual information is available. It can take a bit of practice to learn how to use a player's pause feature efficiently. Some players have a frame-by-frame option (operating both forward and backward) that enables microanalysis of how facial expressions change from one emotion to another. Slow motion also lets you point out to children muscles moving, accentuating how faces change.

Give particular attention to how you arrange the environment, especially for younger children. Children need to be well supported — if they're sitting in chairs, they must sit so their feet are planted. I avoid the entire chair issue by putting the monitor on a low table (mine is a simple, collapsible Asian tea table about 10 inches high). We all sit on the floor using supportive cushions. Students can look straight at the monitor, which is at eye level, while staying in a "strong body" state. This particularly benefits younger children.

Regulatory Aids

As discussed in more detail in Chapter 3, depending on the needs of your students, there are a number of tools you may wish to have at hand before hitting the Play button.

- Visual aids to represent arousal state (see Kuypers, *The Zones of Regulation®*, 2011)
- Hand fidgets
- Gum
- Crunchy food (see the parental release for allergy and diet restrictions, Appendix B)

- Bumpy cushions, positioning balls, or firm, supportive cushions (child-size zafu meditation cushions work well)
- Weighted items to wear or hold, such as blankets, vests, or neck cushions
- Zoom Balls for doing large-body movements before watching

Visual Support Materials

Visual aids support students in their Movie Time Social Learning activities, as discussed in detail in Chapter 5. The visual tools that you'll use will vary somewhat based on the level of Mindreader, but generally you'll want to have the following supplies on hand:

- Sticky notes: Get a lot of these. You can use them to write and draw on as labels for place, thought, feeling, motive, and plan, and attach them to the screen, a dry-erase board, or even to yourself or to the students.
- Dry-erase boards: Use large, wall-size (3 x 4 feet) boards for group work and some hand-held ones (11 x 17 or 7 x 9 inches) to track multiple ideas or to give to students for their own drawing and writing. Buy more than you think you'll ever need; you'll find that you use them all.
- Colored pens or markers: Whether you're using the dry-erase board or paper, you can differentiate social aspects by color (e.g., thought bubbles can be blue, feelings can be red, talk bubbles green, and so on).
- A computer and printer: These are for printing the materials on the CD included with this book, including lesson plans for specific suggested movies. You may also photocopy templates and other handouts included in the book.

Introducing the Program to Administrators, Staff, and Families

Before beginning to use Movie Time Social Learning, take time to outline the program to administrators, other teachers and relevant staff, and students' families. Explain the benefits of working with material that you can freeze and then discuss as a way to cement knowledge that students can then apply in more spontaneous situations. Describe the specific mediating strategies you'll use and how those allow for longer and more detailed conversations about social interactions. Also be prepared to provide administrators, IEP teams, and families detailed goals and information about how you'll monitor progress.

Obtaining Parental Releases

Before you begin the Movie Time Social Learning program, make sure to have participating students' parents sign necessary releases, templates for which are included in Appendix B and on the CD that accompanies the book. These are a permission slip for watching the movies, a release to video record students during sessions (if desired), and a permission form for serving food to students. You may use these as is or customize them to meet your needs.

Ben: Can we watch No Roses for Harry *again today?*
Jake: You stop it all the time, but I still want to watch!

Two eight-year-olds coming in for their therapy session

Chapter 3

PLACES Everyone!

Your Role as Mediator

Over the years that I've been experimenting with the ideas that turned into Movie Time Social Learning, I've had many incredible therapeutic moments; times when conversation moved to another level, as students with all sorts of social thinking challenges grasped an idea in a new and different way. In these moments, children realize something new about themselves.

Your role as mediator is a crucial one: to encourage students to attend to, analyze, and understand the information presented in movies so they can integrate this social knowledge within the context of all their social cognitive work and, ultimately, in their lives.

The usage of the terms "mediator" and "mediating strategies" here is based on the idea of Mediated Learning Experiences (MLE) as developed by the cognitive psychologist Reuven Feuerstein (Feuerstein, 2000). An MLE involves a mediator (such as a teacher, therapist, or parent) helping a learner to organize information and make sense of the world. This facilitation can take a number of forms, including helping learners to:

- Identify and attend to the relevant/salient information
- Understand the meaning of the information
- Extrapolate relevance to other situations (generalize)
- Become more competent in organizing the world for themselves

Mediated learning takes place in a dynamic social relationship, in which the facilitator guides the learners in discovering and exploring connections. This book presents a structured program and ideas to make the job easier, but there's no clear rule book of responses to the many ways a discussion may go. As is true for the students, practice makes it easier to offer the "just right" amount of guidance.

This chapter provides general information about the mediator's role: how to assist students to regulate before they begin watching, ways to help them maintain attention, when to intervene, and when you need to take a break. The chapters that follow this one discuss specific mediating strategies you can use with Movie Time Social Learning: nonverbal or "body-based" strategies (such as silence and gestures), visual aids such as thought bubbles and emotions strips, and verbal tools (such as open-ended questions and restating).

Regulation Before Expectation

Early in my work with Movie Time Social Learning, I had (I believed) settled in with a group of middle-school students to watch a scene from Harry Potter and the Order of the Phoenix. *I paused the movie and asked an insightful question. One child abruptly announced, "Oh, I forgot to get some gum," and moved toward the gum basket, and then I watched as the two other students abandoned the group — one to get a drink, one a favored fidget toy. It took a couple of minutes to settle everyone back down. Um ... which scene were we watching?*

Had I been aware that one of the first steps for success is making sure the children are comfortable, I would have taken a bit more time *before* starting the movie to make sure everyone was ready to begin. As with many children with social learning challenges, the students you're working with may have sensory regulatory and tone issues including:

- Overarousal and/or underarousal
- Difficulty maintaining a well-regulated state
- Sensory-seeking behaviors
- Hypersensitivities
- Low core/torso strength

Watching a movie in a school or clinical setting or even at home can be a very exciting idea, and students who tend to overarouse may need support in reaching and maintaining a level of arousal that's conducive to Movie Time activities. You may already know of regulatory aids that are helpful for a particular child, or you may want to ask for suggestions from the student's parents or occupational therapist. You can then have any materials needed in advance (see Chapter 2 for examples). I often start with large-body activities before we watch, perhaps partnered wheelbarrow walking, Zoom Ball, "Simon Says," or yoga. The proprioceptive feedback and expenditure of energy from such actions help students to remain regulated during sedentary tasks.

Also make sure you've arranged the environment in the best way for your students. If they're sitting in chairs, make sure their feet are planted. With younger children, it's a good idea to have the monitor at their eye level. They may also be helped by wearing or holding weight while they watch, such as blankets, vests, or neck cushions.

While You Watch

Some students may have had bad experiences with dark theaters, loud soundtracks, or constant reminders to "be quiet." They may even be somewhat fearful of movies — they may startle easily or be confused by striking images. They may have found movies confusing or frustrating because the processing load is too great for them.

At the same time, students with social learning deficits may process physical humor and inappropriate behavior with surprising ease. For example, most children are amused by the crude humor in *Shrek*, such as the numerous references to flatulence and some questionable language. They may even find this especially amusing (and that means deregulating).

To address these possible challenges, start slow, with short sessions, and know your movies in advance. This includes deciding what scenes to show or to skip. Depending on the age and development level of the student or group, the parts of a movie you show and stop to discuss will vary greatly. (In the movie scenes discussed in the lesson plans included on the CD, alerts ! indicate particular scenes or portions of scenes that you may want to skip based on your clinical judgment.)

One of our tasks is to explain why particular behaviors are unexpected in the situation — and how to determine where the line in the social sand lies. Many scenes provide excellent opportunities to discuss socially expected and unexpected behaviors, based on contextual judgments and behaviors. However, at times, it's okay and even reasonable to use distracting talk or the fast forward button to gloss over parts of scenes.

"We're Experiencing Technical Difficulties"

Nothing beats a good freeze-frame, one that captures the emotional intent behind the action. However, it can be tricky to pause at just the right moment; you may need to watch closely for the visual element that comes right before the behavior you want to capture. If you make a mistake, it's all right to use your seeming incompetence as a teachable moment: "Yikes, that's all blurry. Let me back it up quickly to see if we can see his face."

Technical glitches can be frustrating for everyone, especially when expectations are high about watching a movie. Nothing is more trying than, with one accidental push of a finger, you reset the movie to the beginning in a DVD that's not subdivided into scenes and then must fast-forward through the whole movie to get to the original spot. I've done this more times than I like to admit. Don't be too hard on yourself when this happens, and present it to the children as an opportunity to express empathy for your struggle!

Students may become upset with all the pausing — after all, they're used to watching movies in a continual stream. Also, they'll learn quickly that a paused scene means they have to work. Be reassuring but firm. For some students (or on "one of those days"), bring in some visual supports. Set a Time Timer (see Appendix C) for a short period or draw out a number of boxes to indicate how much work needs to be completed. This will help children understand that the amount of time they'll be working with Movie Time Social Learning is limited as they come to realize that pausing and talking is actually fun. While most will be willing to try out this new style of movie watching, you may also hear questions and comments such as:

- "Why are you stopping it?"
- "When do we get to *watch* the movie?"
- "Stop hitting the Pause."
- "I don't want you to hit the Pause again."
- "Just hit Play!"

You can respond:

- "We're going to watch it like this for a bit."
- "When I pause it, we can figure out what's happening."
- "We'll watch a bit the regular way later."
- "Yeah, this is a new/different way to watch, isn't it?"

Note: Children like to push buttons. *Do not* give over control of the player, even if they promise they'll "stop it right when you say." Not only is it very hard to actually pause at the correct moment, it's also too much fun to play with the controls.

As you watch movies, you'll undoubtedly be faced with moments when the behavior of the student(s) becomes less than exemplary. Whether it's too much talking, nudging, or giggling, always be ready with your gentle reminders about "we" thinking, zone checks, or whole body listening — changes in social thinking come slowly and need many reminders!

Watching Movies with Varsity Mindreaders

Varsity Mindreaders tend to be older and have more advanced language skills than Moving Up or Junior Mindreaders. They usually have opinions that they want to make known, but they're still working on being able to listen respectfully to the (often differing) ideas of others. Finally, because many of them are teenagers, these students can be challenging to manage, especially in groups of three or four.

Most Varsity Mindreaders enjoy movies and have watched many, probably even the movies you choose for Movie Time Social Learning. You need to balance spontaneity (which you want to encourage) with order, because it's difficult to organize conversation if everyone is calling out during a "lively" discussion. Remind students that with greater age comes greater social responsibility. Some of my most animated discussions have happened with Varsity Mindreaders as they gleefully wallow in social engagement. They're really getting the hang of it, so be prepared for that social exuberance! When using Movie Time Social Learning with older students, just as with younger ones, you'll need to continue working on general Social Thinking ideas, including expected/unexpected behavior, whole body listening, and thinking with your eyes. In other words, you'll be continuing to work on those crucial social cognitive abilities so important to success in the real world.

Mediating with Flexibility

Movie Time Social Learning offers ample and varied activities to foster social cognitive growth. Because the program has built-in flexibility, any one activity can go in several different directions. Similarly, the mediating strategies that you use — which will vary with the students' Mindreader level — can lead down many paths of social learning. This ensures that the work doesn't become "just watching movies."

With practice you'll recognize when it's appropriate to provide mediated intervention, such as in these situations:

- You feel students are "stuck" and unsure where to go with their thinking.
- You want to mediate more complex language you feel students are capable of formulating, given appropriate support.
- You want students to delve into feelings in a way they're not accustomed to doing.
- The situation to be described is challenging to the children or out of their personal experience.
- You want to foster a back-and-forth discussion of socially based ideas rather than a limited interchange of statement/question/statement/end of discussion.
- You'd like to keep the conversation on track and organized around students' own ideas, feelings, and plans, or those of the movie characters.

I find the biggest challenge when using Movie Time Social Learning with children is ... *me!* As therapists, teachers, and other professionals, we love to help, but our best intentions can be counterproductive. We may at times jump in too quickly when students are thinking, reject a solution the students come up with because it wasn't the one we were thinking of, fail to look at their reasoning, or offer solutions perhaps veiled as suggestions.

The point of mediating during Movie Time Social Learning is to work together with students to develop an answer. The more you're able to be a flexible thinker, the easier it will be to take students' perspective and figure out where their social reasoning is stuck. To help students find ways to move forward while watching movies, you can:

- Look where they're looking on the screen
- Watch their expressions to see where the confusion starts
- Restate what they're saying to confirm to them and yourself that you understand what they're thinking
- Constantly strive to discover what each child is thinking
- Explore more than one strategy to reach a goal
- When appropriate, move on to a different task, a different scene, or a different activity altogether

When watching movies with students who have limited social awareness, the possibilities for social confusion are seemingly infinite. Although you may have planned specific Social Thinking activities for a particular scene, such as ones suggested in this book, the dynamic process of Movie Time Social Learning means a session may go in a different direction from the one you (or I) had in mind. That's okay, even good. It means you're being flexible and molding your application of the program to fit the needs of those students.

It's not unusual for a discussion of a segment to take a half-hour or even more. Of course, if you have time limitations, you can cover just part of the scene or choose only the portions you feel are most applicable and interesting to the child or group.

When to Call It a Day

There will come times in sessions when you (as well as the students) will feel stuck. No matter how hard you've tried, it seems as if all the roads you go down turn into dead ends. Perhaps you find yourself losing your patience, the children beginning to deregulate or show in other ways that they can't do it anymore, or you have no idea how to explain the concept in any other way. Call it a day, change to a lighter task, and try another time.

When this happens, I tell children that they've worked hard (which they have), that "sometimes taking a break makes it easier to finally figure out how things work," and that "this can be tricky/hard/challenging to figure out." I tell them that we'll give it another try next time. When we return to the same spot the next day or week, we're often able to get through.

Between sessions, you can try to identify the "stuck point." Usually, it's overload — just too much talking and thinking about feelings and social behavior. You can keep whatever visual supports you've been using and bring them out the next time. If, at the next sitting, the group is at the same frustration point, you may want to take a break from that movie and task, back up to an easier movie with simpler tasks, or take a week or two off from movie watching to do other Social Thinking activities if you're doing Movie Time Social Learning as part of a Social Thinking program.

MOVIE TIME Social Learning Dos and Don'ts

Do... work in consecutive sessions to keep the momentum going as well as remembering the story.

Do...tell students the purpose of the work — identifying thoughts, labeling feelings, tracking changes, and following friendships.

Do...review previous work and movie segments each session.

Do...start using Movie Time in individual sessions or groups of no more than two until you "get the hang of it."

Do...remember the specific Social Thinking goals you are working on. Allow for discussions not directly related to the movie but that address what you're working on (such as contrasting perspectives, empathy, changes in feelings, etc.).

Don't...forget to get children regulated before you start.

Don't ...give over control of the clicker!

Don't...assume knowledge.

Well-timed silence hath more eloquence than speech.

—**Martin Farquhar Tupper**

Chapter 4

QUIET on the Set!

Silence and Other Nonverbal Mediating Strategies

This chapter focuses on body-based, nonverbal mediation strategies that you can use with Movie Time Social Learning: silence, listening to intonation, pacing, gestures, and facial expressions. These are powerful tools, with no batteries required.

Silence

One of the most helpful mediating strategies is silence. Rather than a time to be filled, silence is a time to be used. In developing Movie Time Social Learning, I've been struck not only by what I do to encourage social thinking but also by what I *don't* do. Not talking is at the top of my list. In this program, students are guided to use their social detective skills, to think with their eyes, and focus on details that may be novel and challenging for them and that will take time. Make sure not to interrupt students' processing by talking — make yourself wait, sometimes for a long time. Perhaps allow yourself a drawn-out "hmmm," but respect the students' thinking. Every moment of a session doesn't need to be filled with talking.

If students are scanning or studying the frame or movie, I assume they're thinking. If I note they're simply staring at the screen, I may not make that assumption and might say something. However, when I do decide they're thinking, I don't want to interrupt and I respond with silence. When children look at me, however, I usually interpret this as a request for a cue. This is in large part what we want — they're looking at me! Typically, I start by using silence (which I may accompany with a shrug and encouraging smile), perhaps looking from them back to the screen, which communicates that the answer is there, I have confidence that they can figure it out, and they don't have to hurry up to "just say something — anything."

A Slow Pace

Pacing is another valuable nonverbal strategy to use with students. Especially in early Movie Time Social Learning work, I monitor myself carefully to keep in sync with the students' pace. No one likes to be rushed or feel overwhelmed, particularly when wrestling with new, challenging material. Sometimes I move so slowly I feel as if I'm doing tai chi. I find when I slow down, I get a better sense of how the students are processing and seeing the world.

Listening to Intonation

You can glean much information by listening to students' intonation patterns. These tell you when a student is asking a question or is unsure, when he's telling, and when he's finished. (Intonation is also a tool that I use in my own verbal strategies, as discussed in Chapter 6.)

If you listen well, you know from the intonation patterns when someone has finished verbalizing a thought. How you respond to students' utterances will be based on your assessment of the intonation (see Figure 4.1). (An utterance is a bunch of words bounded by silence and isn't always a completed thought.) If the child is pausing, do nothing. If the child has made a statement or finished talking, you can take your turn. If the child asks a question, even by intonation (e.g., "it's coming out" said with rising intonation to question the statement's accuracy) or uses a statement to reflect uncertainty or confusion, respond with a verbal answer, or perhaps point to where the answer might be found. If a student indicates by rising intonation that he wants to keep talking, don't interrupt, even when he pauses.

If the child's intonation is...	that means she might be...	and you should...
Stretched out at the end of the utterance	Thinking	Wait
Rising at the end of the utterance	Feeling uncertain or wanting to continue or asking a question	Make sure she's asking you a question; answer only if you are sure, otherwise wait
Falling at the end of the utterance	Finishing her statement or is ready to stop talking	Take a talking turn

Figure 4.1. Mediating responses to different intonation patterns

Even small differences in intonation and timing can be important. Figure 4.2 gives several contrasting examples of utterances in which a student clearly finishes one thought at a time and utterances that show development of a thought.

Thoughts communicated through discrete utterances	Development of more complex thought over time
1. It's a dog . . . a dog on the table. (intonation falling)	**1.** It's a dog. . . (intonation rising) It's a dog. . . (intonation rising) A dog. . . (intonation continuing) On the table. . . (intonation continuing) It's a dog on the table. (intonation clearly falling)
2. Park. . .. he's at the park. (intonation falling)	**2.** Park. . . (intonation rising) The park... (intonation continuing) He's at the park. (intonation falls)
3. I like that because it has cute flowers on it. (intonation falling)	**3.** I like that... (intonation rising) I like the flowers... (intonation rising) I like that 'cuz... (intonation continuing) I like that 'cuz... (intonation continuing) 'Cuz... (intonation continuing) I like that 'cuz the flowers are pretty. (intonation falling)

Figure 4.2. Examples of intonation communicating when a student is formulating or has finished a thought

A good rule of thumb: If you have any reason to believe that the student is in the middle of thinking, *wait*. At worst, there will be a pause and there will be silence for a moment.

Gesture

Along with silence and listening to intonation, other active nonverbal techniques such as gesture and facial expressions are equally powerful tools in Social Thinking mediation. The visual channel, which tends to be stronger than the auditory channel in children with social cognitive deficits, can be used to support processing, memory, sequencing, and formulation.

Gesture is an important nonverbal as well as a visual strategy to use with Movie Time Social Learning. Although we may not immediately think of gesture when considering visual cues, gestures help to organize thoughts and language and reinforce communication and connection. Gestures are also a valuable way to provide information. For example, if, to describe a roller coaster ride, I raise my hand to the height of my shoulder and swoop it down, with a fancy twist at the end, I'll have explained the ride more clearly than if I'd used a long string of verbal descriptors. I've demonstrated my internal conceptualization of "roller coaster" — starts high, swoops fast, twists, and curves.

Susan Goldin-Meadow, a researcher at the University of Chicago studying the role of gesture in cognition, development, and linguistics, suggests that "not only is gesture an integral part of communication, but it may also be an integral part of thinking" (Goldin-Meadow, 2003). The importance of gesture has come a long way since I was a student in the 1970s, when waving hello and goodbye was barely mentioned!

Providing gestural support gives students opportunities to think about us and listen with their eyes. To process gestures, we need to at least be oriented toward and visually aware of the person with whom we are talking. This can serve an important function in expanding Social Thinking abilities. Figure 4.3 shows examples of how gestures can be a tool for cuing and expressing conceptual information in Movie Time Social Learning. (Hesitations on the part of the child's formulation are marked with ellipses.) I mediate these with gestures rather than verbally. In addition to expanded language between the first and third columns, the student's addition of a gesture communicates verbal-linguistic and gestural-conceptual information. In the example, with no verbal interruption on my part, the child demonstrates more sophisticated social understanding.

To mediate continued narrative given the student's formulation...	I mediate with no words but the gesture...	and the student continues...
1. "...so he went, he went, so he..."	1. point my finger up	1. "...so he went up in the air" (swooshes arm up)
2. "...he's looking for it..."	2. arms out, palms up in "don't know" posture	2. "but he doesn't know where it is" (shakes head)
3. "there..."	3. palm down over other fist (sign "on")	3. "It's on the table." (points to screen)
4. "He tried to get on."	4. right palm down, turns over (on the other hand...)	4. "He tried to get on but the driver said no. He had to get off." (hand makes "get off" gesture)
5. "It's gonna be big."	5. index finger and thumb indicate "small" (I look confused)	5. "No, not big, it's gonna be a small one." (shakes head "no")

Figure 4.3. Examples of mediating verbal expression using gestural cues

You can encourage students to be aware of the gestures you use as well as *their* ability to use gesture. In my observations of students with social learning differences, I've noticed that they hardly ever use their hands spontaneously. If they don't respond to one of your gestures, you might cue them with: "My hands are telling you..." When you feel their use of gesture might be appropriate, you might cue them: "Show me with your hands" or "Use your hands to help tell me." When students do interpret and use gestures, you can note this and make comments such as, "You figured out what my hands were telling you," or "Wow — when you used your hands I knew just what you meant." Gesture work can be supplemented with charade-type games at other times in sessions.

A discussion of gesture wouldn't be complete without talking about pointing. As a means of establishing joint attention, using various types of nonverbal points allows you opportunities to practice an important channel of social communication. As you begin to incorporate pointing into your work with a particular student, observe carefully to ascertain that student's level of facility with understanding your pointing. Like other work on gesture, you can use tasks in your general Social Thinking work to build processing of pointing in real time. As it applies to Movie Time Social Learning, pointing to the screen can efficiently cue relevant information. This can be a static point, a moving point to find and follow a character's gaze, or an encircling point.

I use static and moving points most with Junior Mindreaders, who are working to understand the social implications of contextual cues and basic relationships between characters. A static point works well to call attention to a relevant visual feature onscreen, as in Figure 4.4. Pointing to visual choices (e.g., emotions strips, conjunction lists, and sentences written down from students) can provide organizing information without verbal interruption. (These types of visual aids are discussed in the next chapter.)

Freeze-frame	Mediating point	Student says
Boy is getting on the bus. **Movie Time prompt:** Silence. Wait for child to say something about character or context. Child says, "Boy."	I point to the bus.	"On the bus. He's getting on the bus."

Figure 4.4. Use of a static point with a Junior Mindreader

Moving points communicate information about connection, whether between two or more characters or between characters and objects. Your hand movement draws an invisible line, encouraging the child to look beyond a single visual feature, as in Figure 4.5.

Freeze-frame	Mediating point	Student says
Winnie the Pooh is searching for honey. **Movie Time prompt:** "What's Winnie thinking about?" Child says, "His house."	I point from Winnie toward the honey pot.	"He's looking for his honey."

Figure 4.5. Use of a moving point with a Junior Mindreader

An encircling point is a broader gesture indicating a larger area to be noticed (e.g., *all* the students in the *classroom*). I use this type of gesture frequently with all Mindreaders (Figure 4.6).

Freeze-frame	Mediating point	Students says
Students are in a classroom. **Movie Time prompt:** "What's happening?"		
Child says, "They're in there."	My index finger goes around the perimeter of the frame, circling the entire room.	"Oh, they're in Umbridge's classroom — it's the first day."

Figure 4.6. Use of an encircling point with a Varsity Mindreader

Encourage and watch for pointing gestures *by the student.* A boy looking from the screen to an emotions strip as he points to the strip indicates that he has internalized the availability and purpose of the aid. This should signal you to pull back from pointing or cuing attention to the strip or to a feelings list, allowing him to then verbally state his conclusion. When you notice a child gesturing, recognize this as part of the formulation process and don't verbally interrupt.

Facial Expression

In an even more sophisticated way, facial expressions can provide mediating visual cues, reflecting emotional states and opinions. Facial expressions can provide subtle cues, communicating to the student whether you feel she's on a path toward understanding (you smile or nod) or a path toward confusion (you look confused or shake your head "no" very slightly).

Reflect alertness, patience, and confidence to reinforce that you're actively listening and waiting. Movie Time Social Learning tasks can be challenging, and children appreciate your support. There's no better way to practice interpersonal relatedness and shared understanding than through synchronous facial expressions. This interpersonal experience of shared enjoyment, while not part of the formal instruction, is something that usually is experienced spontaneously by participants during Movie Time Social Learning tasks.

With all of the strategies discussed in this chapter, you may find that you (and the students you work with) travel a learning curve — you and they may not be accustomed

to so much silence, facial expression, and gesture! Being silent removes much of the information that children with social cognitive challenges depend on, requiring them to look elsewhere (e.g., you) for information. Be patient with them and yourself. Try to incorporate these strategies into all your social cognitive work, and over a short period of time everyone will become accustomed to the new opportunities. This chapter has emphasized the silent and nonverbal aspects of shared communication within the Movie Time Social Learning experience. The next chapter discusses using concrete visual aids to support social learning.

To write is to "paint" with words in the mind of another person.

– **Carol Gray**

Chapter 5

MARK Up Those Cue Cards!

Knowing How to Help Visually

Movie Time Social Learning requires that students manipulate complex information as they work to better understand relationships and social events. As they participate, they have to attend to context, people's words, facial expressions, and more. Concrete visual aids such as those discussed in this chapter help children keep their ideas in working memory as they strive to explain them and explore the workings of the social world. They support students in building their Social Thinking vocabulary, expanding their understanding of how social events are related, and extending and adding to the complexity of discussions.

Verbal language, gestures, and facial expression discussed in the previous chapter offer important but fleeting input, while pictures and writing provide more enduring information. Think about how many visual aids we use in our lives — to organize and chunk information as well as connect ideas.

During Movie Time Social Learning tasks, you'll find yourself drawing and writing for many purposes, such as:

- To track feelings, thoughts, and plans
- To expand students' language narrative
- To organize thoughts and opinions during discussions

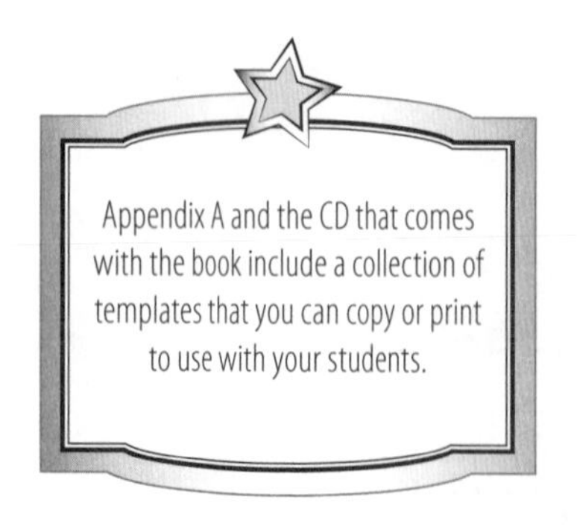

The ease of erasing and using color makes dry-erase boards a great medium for both you and students. It's a lot easier to redo a sketch after a quick erase than to sweat with a crumbly eraser. If I want to keep a piece of work, I copy or take a photo of it with my phone.

Visual information that you write or draw in the moment can be supplemented with prepared materials, kept within easy reach, that you anticipate using frequently. Appendix A and the CD that comes with the book include a collection of templates that you can copy or print to use with your students. These materials include emotions strips, lists of conjunctions, and a variety of templates for tracking different aspects of the student work.

Using Pictures and Symbols—Especially for Junior Mindreaders

Most children with social cognitive challenges are visual learners. Junior Mindreaders work very well with sketches, although if they're readers they can also work with clearly written text. Thought, feeling, and plan bubbles can be drawn on sticky notes and placed directly onto the screen or monitor. Sketches easily summarize and organize multiple characters, whether added to the screen or drawn on a separate surface. Making such thoughts and feelings visible helps young children figure out what's happening with the movie's characters.

Fortunately, children don't require elaborate artwork. For a young nonreader, a visual aid for a thought bubble for *Frog Goes to Dinner* showing what the boy is thinking about when he studies the menu might look like this:

Used with permission by Weston Woods, © 1985 by Evergreen Productions

Figure 5.1. A drawn thought bubble for a Junior Mindreader *(Frog Goes to Dinner)*

You may choose to work on only one aspect of a social event (e.g., feelings) or with any combination (e.g., feelings and thoughts), depending on how much the students can handle at once. When two or more characters have different opinions about the same thing, visual aids can help students keep these multiple thoughts straight. Constructing both feeling and thought bubbles implies that, although they function closely together, feelings and thoughts can be discussed separately to explore the connection between them. In the example in Figure 5.2 from *No Roses for Harry*, thought bubbles show contrasting feelings and perspective — the kids are happy and like the sweater, while Harry is mad and doesn't like the gift. Such a visual aid might look like this:

Figure 5.2 Junior Mindreader thought bubbles *(No Roses for Harry)*

Visual aids can also show a character's plan, as in this example:

Figure 5.3. Plan bubble used with Junior Mindreaders *(No Roses for Harry)*

Pictures and symbols can also give students a road map as they explore the "who" and the "where" of scenes and focus on "getting the big picture." With Junior Mindreaders in particular, you'll spend quite a bit of time talking about context since it is from context that we draw many social cues. (See Chapter 7 for more information about Spy Eye activities.) Context, or the "where," can be difficult for the students to identify; they may say a character is "eating a cracker" rather than looking at the larger context of "eating snack at school." To understand the social implications of a scene, it's helpful to identify the larger picture. Eating a cracker is less important than social engagement with peers during snack time.

Similarly, identifying the "who" of social scenes is key to identifying the relationships between individuals as well as overall context. A student with social learning differences may identify a woman in a picture as a "mom" without recognizing that she's in a classroom leading a group of children, and is therefore actually a "teacher" in that context.

Simple line drawings or pictures you sketch or compose using computer programs can support students as they search for contextual information. Just pointing to or gesturing toward the symbols or sketches, without a verbal interruption, guides the child to focus on the larger picture in a more observant way and reference that information through language.

You may already have pictures or icons as part of other programs that you use with students. One popular teaching program you can use in Movie Time Social Learning is the Picture Exchange Communication System (PECS™), developed as an augmentative/alternative communication intervention. Another great program is Maryellen Rooney Moreau's Story Grammar Marker®. This program features appealing and effective icons that are available as visual aids and manipulatives to build oral language and narrative. You can attach a set of the program's magnetic icons to dry-erase boards to use with movie tasks. The character and setting icons work well as a visual aid to identify the "who" and the multiple aspects of the "where." More information on Story Grammar Marker can be found at http://www.mindwingconcepts.com.

I've Got a Feeling

Visual symbols are particularly helpful in working with feelings, which are involved in most Movie Time Social Learning tasks. Depending on the task and level of Mindreader, you can choose from a variety of visual materials to make abstract feelings more concrete. Students can identify feelings with an emotions strip, describe the intensity of feeling with a scale, or explore how a feeling changes using a continuum.

Emotion Strips

When working on the identification of feelings with Junior Mindreaders, I typically provide support with either a basic four emotions strip (sad, happy, angry/mad, and okay) or an expanded six emotions strip that also includes afraid/scared and surprised. Such visual representations are incredibly helpful for students with social cognitive deficits who typically are inexperienced at labeling their own and others' feelings.

Figure 5.4. Basic four emotions strip template

At the start of such work, some children are unable or unwilling to name the emotions, especially sad and mad. You can encourage them to begin by pointing to the emotion's picture in the strip and then label it. Some students who are able to point to the correct choice pretty easily prefer to spell out rather than name the emotion. After they can spell it, you might move to "Can you write it?" Because many students who can spell the word are reasonable writers, you can finally move to "Can you read that word?" and "You read the feeling word 'sad.'" Through this nonthreatening process, going at the pace of the child, conversation about feelings can begin.

Feeling Continua and Scales

With all levels of Mindreaders, you can help guide understanding of how feelings change (sometimes rapidly) over even short periods of time by mapping these shifts visually, such as with a feeling continuum. Horizontal continua can be used to represent changes in feelings relative to events or other characters. (You can refer to *Navigating the Social World* by Jeanette McAfee for more information about using horizontal continua.) All Mindreaders need to practice making these rapid judgments, as well as explain the reasons behind the shifts. These continua are particularly helpful to contrast how two characters can have different feelings at the same time.

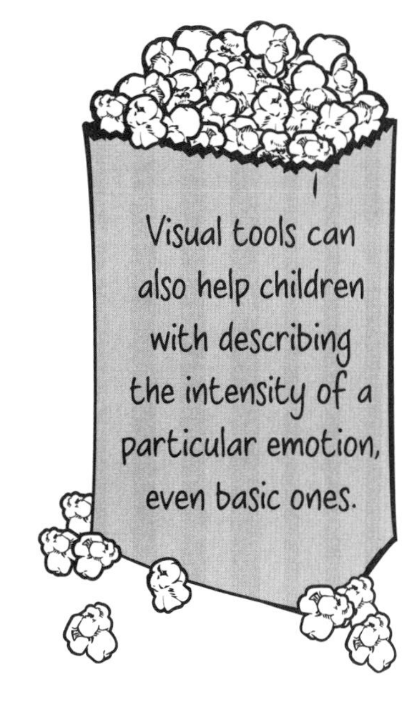

Visual tools can also help children with describing the intensity of a particular emotion, even basic ones. All "mad" is not the same. Annoyed, frustrated, and furious are discrete labels for emotions in the "mad" category. Even young Junior Mindreaders can make judgments describing the relative size of an emotion. With them I use a three-point scale of size using small, medium and big circles. You can supplement this with gestures, displaying size with your fingers as well.

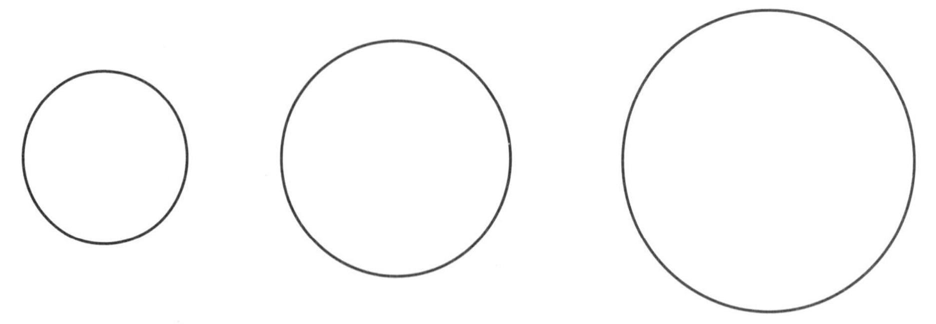

Figure 5.5. Three-point scale for size of feelings

With Moving Up and Varsity Mindreaders, you can also show the size of a feeling by using a vertical scale from 1 to 5 such as in *The Incredible 5-Point Scale* by Kari Dunn Buron and Mitzi Curtis. Take time to assign emotion labels to each of the numbers or points on the continuum. These continua are particularly helpful to contrast how two characters can have different feelings at the same time.

Using Lists and Other Written Language

All levels of Mindreaders who are reading can work with the written word in addition to sketches and scales. As shown in the following examples, you can create thought bubbles, track thoughts and feelings, or list individual traits when comparing and contrasting movie characters.

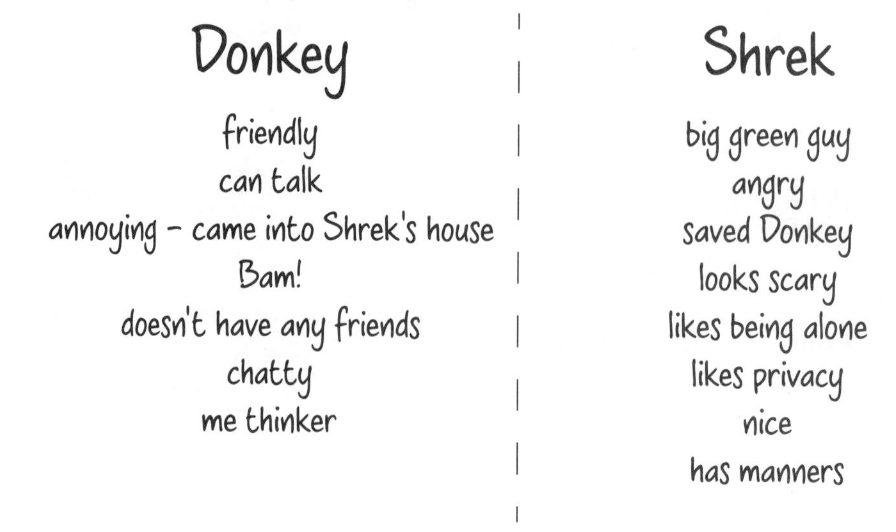

Figure 5.6. Contrasting traits with Moving Up Mindreaders (*Shrek*)

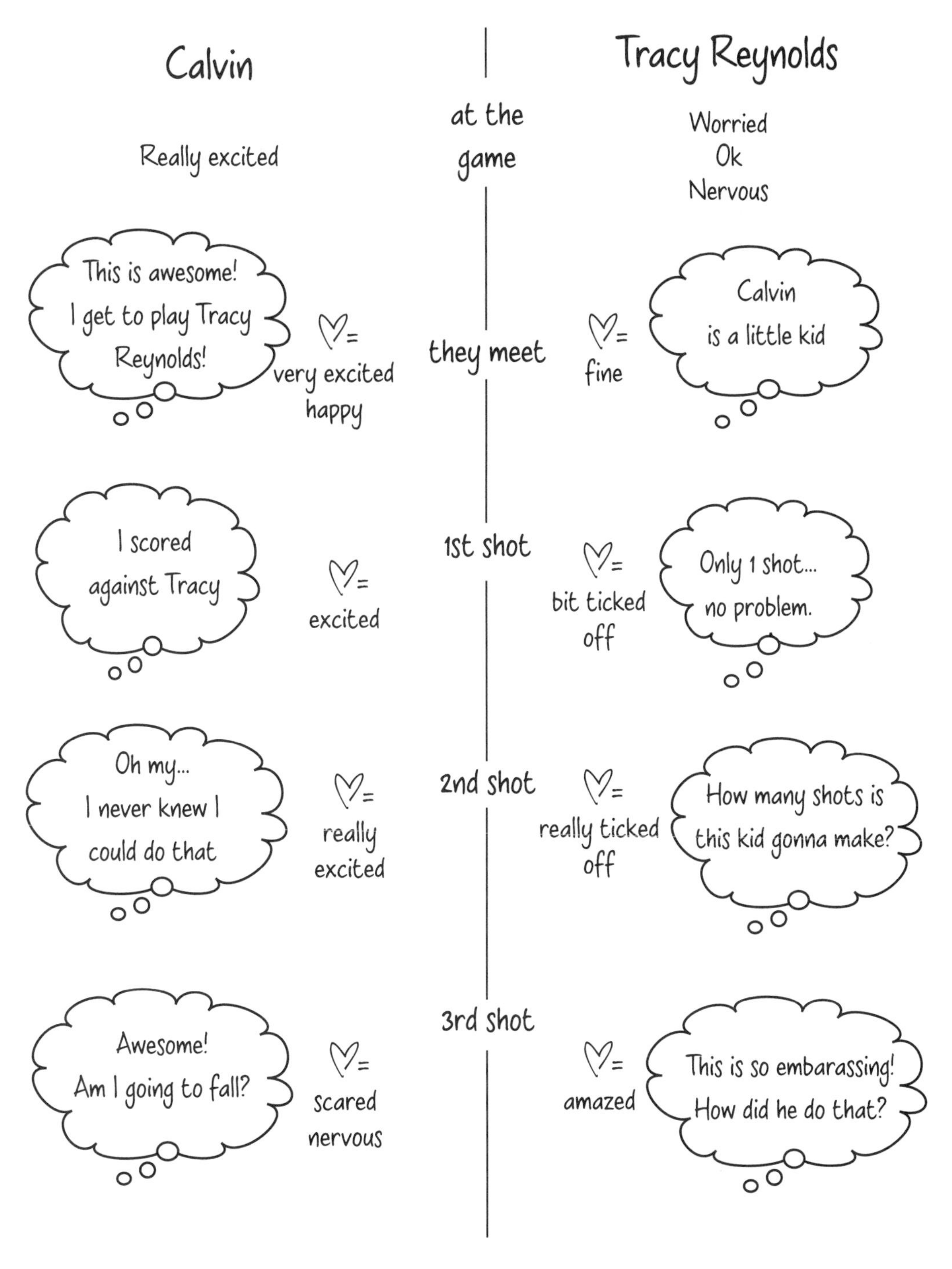

Figure 5.7. Tracking contrasting thoughts and feelings of two characters within a scene with Moving Up Mindreaders (*Like Mike*)

With more advanced tasks that track relationships or look at how events influence motives, visual products will get bigger and more complicated. As you tackle complex relationship ideas, additional social information will develop that can be visually recorded. You may believe that older students don't need much visual support, but remember that most of the students you work with have executive function challenges and need outside help to organize their thinking, particularly when dealing with social information.

Figure 5.8 shows a partially completed product related to the movie, *Harry Potter and the Order of the Phoenix*. The five middle school students are discussing shifting feelings among three main characters during in a scene that involves a hearing. A second chart was developed concurrently to identify the characters' motives (Figure 5.9).

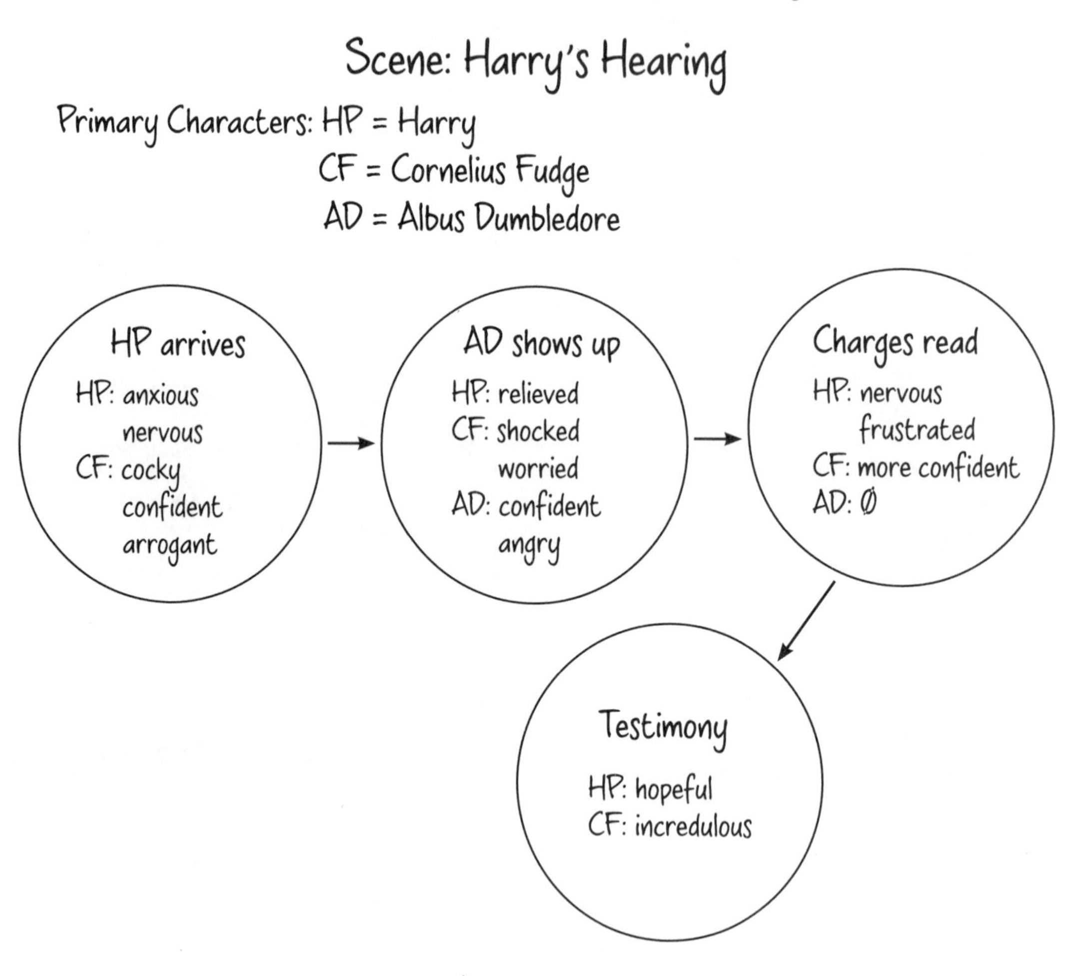

Figure 5.8. Varsity Mindreaders tracking changes in feeling states (*Harry Potter*)

Scene: Harry's Hearing

Primary Characters HP = Harry
CF = Cornelius Fudge
AD = Abus Dumbledore

Motives HP - get acquitted
- return to Hogwarts

AD - help Harry
- win the trial
- challenge Minister

CF - get HP kicked out of Hogwarts
- beat AD
- show HP is bad

Figure 5.9. Varsity Mindreaders' contrasting motives (*Harry Potter*)

Your final visual products may not be understandable to someone who didn't participate in the discussion. That doesn't matter. What matters is that they're clear to everyone involved.

Lists of Emotions

Many Moving Up and Varsity Mindreaders who are ready to expand their feeling vocabulary won't have had much experience beyond the expanded six (sad, happy, angry, okay, afraid, and surprised). Instead of using emotion strips with images, you can use the strips with six emotions in printed words as provided in Appendix A. You can also use lists of more complex emotions. For examples of complex lists of feelings, refer to *Mind Reading: The Interactive Guide to Emotions* (CD-ROM) by Simon Baron-Cohen and *Navigating the Social World* by Jeanette McAfee. Using lists of feelings adds visual structure to the often novel and challenging task of exploring emotions (e.g., devastated, impatient, suspicious) that students recognize but cannot necessarily retrieve spontaneously.

Using Lists of Conjunctions

To generate complex sentences, most Mindreaders need support in choosing and using appropriate conjunctions (such as "because," "but," and "since") as they describe relationships. Lists of conjunctions can serve as a bridge from simpler to more complex thought. Talking about social events invariably involves conjunctions — forms that help to explain relationships among people, events, or things. We use conjunctions to discuss:

- The influence of context on thoughts
- Feelings developing as a consequence of events
- Motives reflecting personal desires
- Reasons behind social events

After writing them out many times, I compiled two lists: a simpler one for Junior Mindreaders (those who know how to read) and a longer and more sophisticated list for Moving Up and Varsity Mindreaders. Students can refer to these lists as they work to chain together events and explain relationships (see Appendix A). Ways to implement the lists are covered later in this chapter as well as in Chapter 6.

- and
- but
- so
- because
- if

Figure 5.10. Useful conjunctions for Junior Mindreaders

- and
- but
- or
- for
- so
- after
- even if
- until
- although
- even though
- when
- as
- if
- whenever
- as long as
- since
- where
- because
- so that
- while
- before
- unless

Figure 5.11. Useful conjunctions for Moving Up and Varsity Mindreaders

Sometimes when using these lists with groups, I may guide students (by pointing or writing) toward a conjunction I think may help them to complete their thought. But the conjunction I think is a good choice fits because of *my* idea. The children may have different ideas and be formulating thoughts using conjunctions that work for *their* thoughts. Always drop your idea if their thoughts are legitimate, and work to support them in their formulation. Listen to their perspective over yours.

Supporting Social Narrative

Combining ideas about context, thoughts, and plans requires linking together phrases into more sophisticated narrative and explanation. While better language won't directly lead to better social understanding, it does play a role in supporting social cognition (Rooney Moreau, 2011). Your drawn and written visual supports will help students talk about the social world and expand the language they use to describe what's happening.

All the thinking and talking can get pretty dense as students struggle to express their understanding of events and relationships. Dry-erase boards are an ideal tool to keep track of sometimes unwieldy language, which will probably be full of incomplete sentences, garbled sequencing, restarts and revisions, illogical explanations, and errors of all kinds.

Your task is to assist students in chaining thoughts together and expressing them in more detailed and logical ways. Information provided through a permanent visual channel, whether drawn sketches or written language, supports children in developing social reasoning language skills.

Junior Mindreaders who don't read will benefit from your pointing along with drawn visual aids (thought and feeling bubbles, sketches indicating plans). This usually is enough to get them started describing connections between characters and events. When eliciting language, it's easier with many children to work solely through such visual channels; I don't have to say anything. With silence and gestural support turning their focus back to previously generated visual supports, children often use more language than you might think them capable of producing.

Such "visual only" aid is much easier for children who read. I support readers in formulating narrative by writing what they say on dry-erase boards. When I want more complete language, I don't put a period at the end of their statement. Rather, I will choose to write a conjunction I feel might work with their thought, providing a fill-in-the-blank opportunity. Then, I cue the children to read — usually by tapping the place I want them to start. If they fill in the blank with an elaborating phrase, I add it. I may even add another conjunction at that point, if I feel they're able to elaborate more. Each time, I cue them (again by tapping) to read from the beginning of the sentence.

In the example that follows, Eli, a five-year-old Junior Mindreader, develops complex narrative to describe the social context of a scene from *Whistle for Willie*. He's describing a part of the movie where Willie has a plan to trick his dog. Although this event was outside of Eli's personal experience, I thought with mediation he could generate some pretty complex language. Although Eli has significantly limited social thinking skills, he's an excellent reader and writer. I start writing as he speaks, adding conjunctions I feel might be helpful, but Eli quickly takes over writing his part. The italicized words represent my contributions.

> The boy is in the box *because* he likes his dog. He wants to whistle *so* his dog will come *but* he can't whistle so the dog went past the box. The boy feels sad *because* he can't whistle at all.

When children read what I've written, I make sure they read the sentence as it is (a complex thought) rather than as a simple sentence with a phrase tacked on at the end. Their intonation tells me when they conceptualize the sentence as a unit. While Eli may not have totally understood the connections between the events under discussion, his progress over time in using more sophisticated language will make it easier for him to share his social ideas with others. I continue this process until I feel they've done their best to provide enough information.

When the narrative is finished, I sometimes cue them to tell it from the beginning. While this does smack of the "say the whole thing" technique that I usually don't support, it's important for children to experience the feeling of talking out a chunk of language. Children who generally speak with simpler language need to learn how to say a complex sentence — breath support and phrasing are just two of the necessary ancillary skills. They're happy to read their own words out loud; it's one of their strengths. This process can result in surprisingly accurate narrative descriptions.

The Story Grammar Marker program described earlier is a wonderful visual structure to assist, especially those in grades 2-5, in understanding and developing complex social narrative. Specifically, the Critical Thinking Triangle shows the relationships among events, feelings, and resulting plans as children develop their narrative (Figure 5.12).

Let's Get Organized: Um, What Did We Decide?

Identifying and understanding motives and plans of multiple characters requires a broad assortment of skills (memory, sequencing, understanding cause-and-effect, etc.). Students with social cognitive limitations can find this work challenging and frustrating. They have a hard time keeping ideas they may not completely understand in their minds as they think about them. Using tools such as tables, flowcharts, lists, and other visual organizers can support children's reasoning (Figure 5.13).

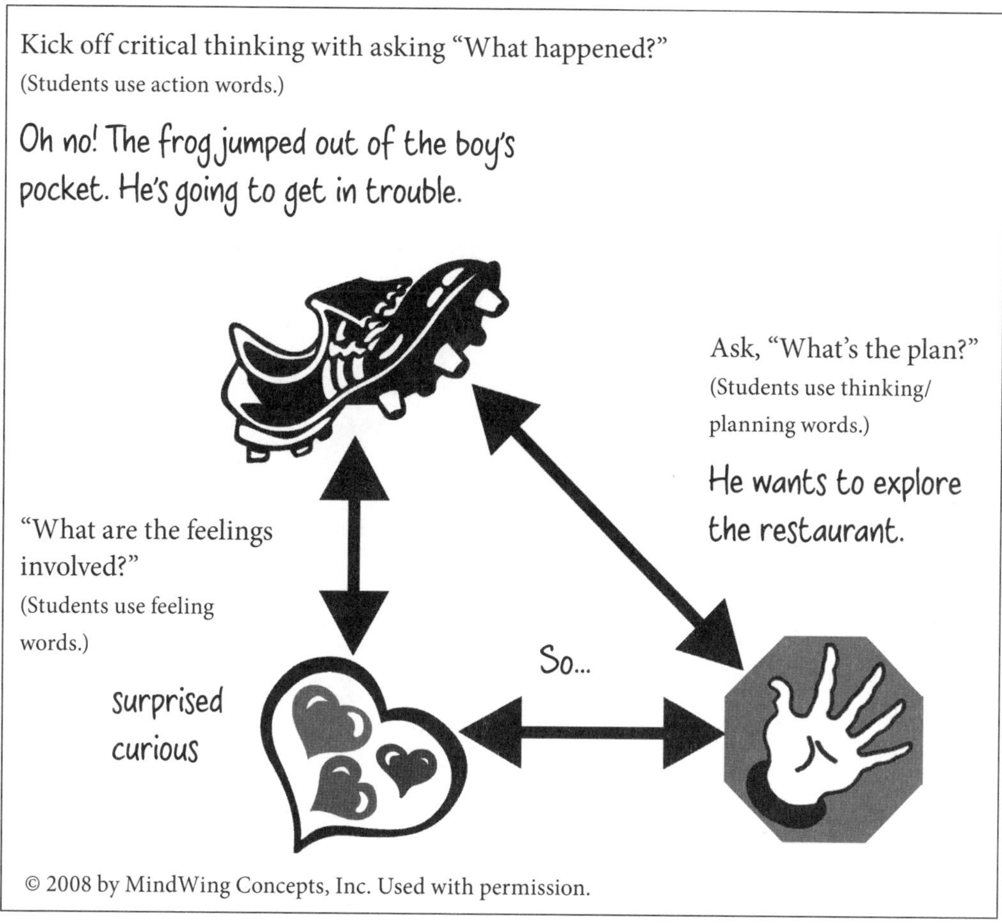

Figure 5.12. Using the Critical Thinking Triangle *(Frog Goes to Dinner)*

Character	Wants	Plan	What finally happens
Boy	To keep his balloon — he likes it	Take it with him wherever he goes, protect it from harm	It gets popped but the boy is okay at the end
Other boys	To get the balloon to play with it	Steal it from the boy and. . .	They get it and pop it

Figure 5.13. Visual organizer to track plans and outcomes (*The Red Balloon*)

In more advanced tasks (Detective Head and Me, Too!), you may find yourself left out of the conversation as two or three Moving Up or Varsity Mindreaders actively discuss and debate without you. This is great! However, you still have a role as an organizer of their thoughts from the periphery. The children will benefit from your serving as note taker: writing thoughts, motives and feelings as they're generated (Figure 5.14).

Patrick wanted to show the boys Boone & Little Bear.

Omni: scared, freaked out

Patrick: excited, happy

Omri stopped Patrick. They argue.

Omri: upset, very freaked out

Patrick: angry

The teacher comes over. He wants Patrick to show what's in the pouch.

Omri: upset, freaked out, frustrated

Patrick: angry he didn't get his way - gonna show the teacher

Patrick realizes Omri really doesn't want Patrick to show the teacher.

Omri: unhappy, freaked out, nervous

Patrick: unhappy, worried, scared (sorry about trying to show Boone & Little Bear to the boys)

Patrick shows the teacher two real toys.

Omri: relaxed, happy

Patrick: relaxed, happy

They make up with each other.

Figure 5.14. Visual organizer to discuss fight between two characters with Moving Up Mindreaders (*The Indian in the Cupboard)*

You can use the tracker templates included with this book in Appendix A and on the CD to help students at all Mindreader levels organize their thinking as they watch. Templates are included for these organizers:

- Idea and Opinion Tracker
- Empathy Tracker
- Opinions Tracker
- Event, Thought, and Feelings Tracker
- Problem and Options Tracker
- Event and Feelings Tracker

Appendix A also includes completed examples of these templates, and the lesson plans on the CD suggest which ones you might want to use with specific movie activities.

Personal Strengths and Handy Technology

As you think about the many ways to use visual strategies to mediate social thought, you'll begin to develop your own style. You may be a fantastic artist or organizer of visual information and may already have developed a set of visual tools. The suggestions presented in this chapter, while they work for me, are only a few of the many possible strategies. The more ways you can be a flexible social thinker, the more you'll begin to develop your own way of using visual aids. Your therapy will always be unique.

In addition to the materials mentioned, you can use a phone or another digital camera to take quick pictures of sessions in progress to support later discussions of expected or unexpected social behaviors (e.g., body positioning, facial expression). You can photograph visual aids that you've developed to use later (it's one way to begin developing templates of your own). In addition, you may want to capture video of group discussions (with written parental consent, as in Appendix B) to document in-the-moment social interaction (balanced discussion, turn taking, use of gesture, success in making one's point, active listening to the opinions of others, etc.) for later discussion with parents as well as students.

There are myriad ways to use visual images to help students with social cognitive difficulties process information, stay focused on the issues being discussed, and move forward in their social understanding. As you use Movie Time Social Learning, you'll undoubtedly find more tools to add to your personal Social Thinking program.

Of course, visual supports don't occur in a vacuum — they're part of lively interactions around (hopefully) motivating movie scenes. The next chapter details effective ways to bring in verbal information to create a complete bundle of mediating strategies.

I never taught language for the purpose of teaching it; but invariably used language as a medium for the communication of thought.

– **Anne Sullivan,** *The Story of My Life*

Chapter 6

DIALOGUE Coaches at the Ready!

Knowing How to Help with Words

When it comes to verbal mediation, there's no simple answer for "How much am I supposed to talk?" There are, however, answers for "What am I supposed to say?" and "Are some things better and more effective to say in eliciting discussions about social thinking?" This chapter looks at language tools you can use to support Movie Time Social Learning discussions, including intonation, open-ended questions, offering verbal cues, using conjunctions, restating, and expressing uncertainty.

When mediating Movie Time Social Learning tasks, I constantly monitor how much I'm talking. I want any words I speak to be clear and concise and I try to make sure anything I say is intentional. This way I avoid interrupting or overwhelming the interpretation of a movie scene with too much language. At times, I even have to press my lips together to stop myself from inserting what I think would be a helpful comment.

Using Language to Encourage Social Thought

In everyday social situations, of course, speakers frequently interrupt each other. We certainly want students with social learning challenges to learn how to "pop in" when they have something to add as well as how to maintain (as is appropriate) their talking turn when interrupted by others. However, during Movie Time tasks, many children struggle to get their words out. This means if you find it necessary to give verbal prompts to start or keep a discussion rolling, you'll want to speak in the Goldilocks tradition — not too little, not too much, but just enough. Don't worry; there are degrees of "just enough." The language you use to mediate will be influenced by several factors for each student or group of students:

- The student's social thinking, processing, and language skills
- The student's mood and level of arousal
- Your mood and level of arousal
- The movie you're watching
- The challenge level of the task
- The student's willingness to work hard
- Your comfort level with letting the student wrestle with difficult concepts

One of our goals, whether we are a therapist or teacher, is to help children use language effectively — similar to what's used casually in the outside world, not language that works only in a clinical setting.

It's easy to fall into the trap of eliciting and encouraging "linguistically complete" language, which can be measured and reported to meet specific goals. While there's nothing wrong with a complete sentence, it's only one way of addressing language expansion. H. Paul Grice, a language philosopher instrumental in the field of pragmatics, understood this pitfall and proposed general principles that govern language use. Two are particularly relevant to this discussion (Grice, 1975):

- Give only the information that's needed by your listener.
- Be brief (nonredundant).

Polar questions should, if the speakers are aware of how to use language appropriately, be answered with a brief, nonredundant yes or no. If one person asks, "Would you like to have some cookies?" and the other person answers, "Yes, I'd like to have some cookies," at some level the first person will feel uncomfortable because the answer was redundant. The questioner will wonder why the other person didn't just say "yes" (or preferably, "yes, please"). When we encourage children to "say the whole thing" in an effort to elicit complete language formulations, we often may sacrifice the overall purpose of communication to meet our measurable goals. Rather, we should teach them to use language according to Grice's rules — efficiently and not redundantly.

As you move through the tasks, pay attention to the discussion structures you hear developing; if things are going well, you'll hear fragments, interruptions, revisions, isolated embedded phrases and, yes, entire sentences. Strive for variety, and remember that language composed only of complete sentences would sound more like a dry lecture than an interesting discussion. Movie Time Social Learning is about interesting discussions that expand social thinking!

Much of your verbal mediation will be trying to make complex social thinking understandable to children who are predisposed to retreat from and be confused by the social world. This is about using language to help explain relational events and break down social moments into clearer sequences. At the same time, you're conveying that social thinking isn't linear in nature; any social moment always has at least one unique element that throws something new into the equation. We need to use flexible language forms for *flexible social thinking*, not rote language for rigid social thinking. The first will serve children well wherever they go; the second will result in robotic and "unreal" social behavior that can be coded by the world as fake, "off," or even weird.

Intonation: Use Your Voice, Not Just Your Words

As discussed earlier in Chapter 4 with regard to listening to students, intonation contours and tone of voice are important aspects of social interaction. In Movie Time Social Learning, these cues come to the student from characters in the movie as well as from you. Notice the difference in the statements "The *mouse* is in the house" and "The mouse is in the *house*." Intonation lets the student know whether "house" or "mouse" is the focus.

Intonation contours and changes in tone during conversation provide an incredible amount of information, especially in animated or heated discussions, as they:

- Denote intensity of feelings ("*Wow*! Thanks *so* much!")
- Accentuate qualifying elements ("They only had *blue* ones left!")
- Carry information about humor or sarcasm ("Oh yes, I absolutely *love* those!")
- Spotlight contextual elements of particular importance ("No, I asked you to buy *wheat* bread!")

When you review movie scenes with this type of discourse, point out contrasting intonations to students and offer cues such as, "Listen to *how* he said it" or "Listen, his voice is telling you *exactly* what he's upset about." This will allow the students, with multiple rewinds if necessary, to notice important elements beyond the words, emphasizing that "*how* we say it" usually is more important than "*what* we say."

As the mediator, you're an important communicator about content as well as emotion. You can modify your intonation to punch up particular words or phrases: "So you're saying that he *doesn't* want his *dad* to know about the Indian because then his dad would probably *take him away*. What do you think his plan will be *now*?" In this example, I combine stressed intonation on certain words or phrases and elongation of certain words with restating (a strategy discussed later in this chapter).

Open-Ended Questions: Your Best Bet

As you progress through the tasks, you'll have particular goals (identify a plan, label a feeling, explain a relationship) for the students. Match your verbal mediation to your goal, but strive to do so with interesting, open-ended language that will allow the children's thoughts and language to lead your mediation. Open-ended questions encourage answers longer than one word. Replace questions that start with "do," "does," "will," "is," and "did" that can be answered with "yes" or "no" with leading questions that start with:

- *Why* do/does/did/is/are/will…
- *When* will/can/should…
- *What* do/does/did/is/are/will…
- *How* will/can/could/should…

These question forms encourage complex thought, explanation, and justification.

Offering Verbal Cues

In Movie Time Social Learning we want students to think in new ways about information they may never have considered or even noticed. This section offers specific ways you can use your language to encourage students to go out on that limb and make and explain their social thinking observations.

Cuing Attention to Contextual Elements

Many of the program's tasks focus on making contextual interpretations. Often you'll want children to notice and think about a feature of the scene they've missed or not interpreted sufficiently. Cue attention to these visual elements with mediation statements such as:

- Think about everyone else.
- Think about where they are.
- I wonder where they are now?
- Think about what's around them.

- Watch how everyone else is listening.
- He sees something important happen — watch carefully.

Cuing Attention to Emotional States

Labeling and discussing feelings are important components of all tasks. In conjunction with visual aids to support these activities (as discussed in the previous chapter), cue thoughts about emotional states with language such as the following statements:

- Watch [X's body/face] — that will tell you how he feels about [event].
- Her feeling is going to change — watch carefully.
- Watch for how his face changes when [event happens]. Let's figure out if his feelings changed.
- Wow, that was [describe event]! I wonder how [X] is feeling?

Thoughts are a starting point for many tasks. To encourage "thought about thought," you may find one of the following variations useful to say:

- I wonder what she's thinking about.
- Think about what he's looking at... What do you think he's thinking about that?
- That's what she's *feeling*; what is she *thinking*?
- What is he thinking about? Remember, figure out where he's looking.

Cuing Attention to Nonverbal Behaviors

Nonverbal behavior offers important social information. Cue attention to nonverbal behaviors with very specific language:

- Watch [X] (character).
- Watch how [X's] body moves and think about what those movements tell you.
- Watch [X's] face — it's going to tell you something important.
- Make sure [X's] body matches what she's saying — remember, it might not.
- Watch [X] when he's listening to [Y]. You'll see [X's] reaction to what [Y] is saying.
- Listen to how [X] says that...

Cuing Attention to Characters' Language

Most movies you choose will contain spoken language, although it can also be interesting to do some viewing with the sound off. Keep in mind your knowledge of the children's language level as you cue attention to characters' language:

- Listen to what the character says.
- Pay attention to her answer.
- Think about what he said; it was important — let's watch again.
- That sounded complicated. Let's watch and listen to that part again.
- How can you explain what she said?

Cuing Attention to Perspective Taking

In Movie Time Social Learning, students are asked to identify and consider multiple perspectives as they develop their social thinking abilities. Use language that focuses on such differences as you cue attention to perspective taking:

- … I'm not sure they're all thinking the same thing…
- Does [X] know that? Does [Y] know that? Do *we* know that?
- I think [X] and [Y] have two different ideas — let's see if we can figure them out.
- [X] looks surprised/shocked/confused. I wonder why?

Cuing Attention to Characters' Planning Process

To help students explore plans and motives, use language that will cue attention to the process of thinking beyond the original thought or feeling into the future. This is a great opportunity to use Social Thinking vocabulary such as the "group plan" and "figuring out other people's plans."I wonder what [Y's] plan is?

- I wonder why he wants that?
- You said [Y] is thinking ________; what do you think she might do next?
- How can he get that to happen?
- Is there a group plan? What is it?
- What does [X] think about [Y's] plan?
- How do you think that will work?
- What would your plan be?

All of these language suggestions can work in many other situations in which you want to encourage deeper thought. To see additional examples of specific types of questions you can use with Movie Time Social Learning tasks, see the lesson plans on the CD.

Conjunctions: Putting Thoughts Together

Conjunctions you can use for visual support were introduced in Chapter 5. Much as you do with written mediation, you can use a verbal fill-in-the-blank or bridge to elicit the embedded phrases required to produce a complex sentence. An example is offered in Figure 6.1. A linking conjunction (see the Conjunctions Lists in Appendix A) can serve as a bridge.

With any type of mediating bridge, however, keep in mind that you're following your own line of thought, which may not be what a student is thinking. You may have a "but" phrase in mind to complete the description, while the child may be leaning conceptually toward a "because" explanation. You may get a response using a different conjunction or a different answer than what you have in mind. Being a flexible-thinking adult mediator is one of the challenging but most enjoyable aspects of Movie Time Social Learning work.

Given a student's limited statement...	I mediate with a fill-in-the-blank conjunction...	And the student continues...
1. The boy didn't see Willie.	1. because...	1. He doesn't know he's in the box. He didn't see him because he doesn't know he's in the box.
2. He doesn't think they can hear him.	2. You think he doesn't know they can't hear him because...	2. He doesn't think they can hear him because you can hear out but not in — he doesn't know that.
3. I dunno.	3. Yeah, I'm not sure either, but...	3. I know — he's gonna jump out 'cuz he doesn't want the lobster to grab him.

Figure 6.1. Mediating complex language by providing bridging conjunctions

Restating: What Did You Just Say?

Restating means summarizing a student's statement. Children often benefit from reviews of their discussion to help them keep track of what they and others have said. Restating allows students to hear a more concise presentation of their thoughts (theirs may have gone all over the map), from which they can move forward. Restating can include rephrasing, moving language around, etc.

Children often spontaneously repeat what I've said, either wholly or in part. In doing so, they may make modifications or corrections as well as errors. If the errors are relevant to the social thinking, I usually restate what I said, placing emphasis on the parts that seem confusing. Particularly in groups, restating can help to continue a discussion once everyone has been caught up to where the conversation ended.

In the following example, two Varsity Mindreaders and I were watching "Occlumency," a dramatic scene from *Harry Potter and the Order of the Phoenix*. At the end of the scene, Jeffrey and Chris have each identified feelings for the characters, but their choices are somewhat in disagreement with each other. I want to generate discussion between the boys, either to reach some consensus or to let each explain his choice and possibly convince the other. Both use intonation as an integral part of their discourse to emphasize particular words and to clarify their point. I used restating as well as intonation in this example.

Movie scene:
Snape begins training Harry to block Voldemort from entering his brain.

Transcription (italics in dialog indicate emphatic intonation):

Anna: Chris, you think Snape is feeling *annoyed* because he hates Harry, and Jeffrey, you think that Snape is *concentrating* hard to teach Harry to keep Voldemort out of his mind — that he's *helping* Harry. Think about all this as we watch again. (*replay scene*)

Jeffrey: See, see, Snape *does* hate Harry, but right then he is *teaching* Harry something he really needs to know. Dumbledore *asked him* to teach him. (*looking at screen*)

Chris: But Snape really *hates* Harry, he really does... (*looking at Jeffrey*)

Jeffrey: Yeah, I know. (*looking at Chris, pointing to screen*) But he's trying to teach him what Harry needs to know. He's *working really hard* — he's not annoyed that Harry isn't learning it. Well, maybe he is *frustrated*, but he knows it's *hard*. He's really focused on Harry 'cuz he knows Voldemort is going to attack his brain.

Chris: Well, yeah... (*body moves back in seat, looks with uncertainty at the screen*) I guess he *is* trying to teach him and it's hard. Yeah, I guess he's frustrated... (*Jeffrey nodding*) Yeah, he's *frustrated*... (*looking at me*)

Anna: Well, you are both saying that right there Snape is *frustrated. But* it is true, he has lots of strong feelings about Harry. (*conversation continues...*)

In this example, Jeffrey was able to consider Snape's personal characteristics within context, recognizing that Snape is able to put his feelings about Harry aside while he teaches him something important. Chris is fixated on the fact that Snape hates Harry and can't move beyond that.

Leave Your Certainty at the Door

Your willingness to be uncertain can lead the students to take risks. Because I say "I wonder..." so much, sometimes I think children in my practice see me as an adult who doesn't make up her mind and is never sure about anything! However, because this simple phrase almost always generates an opinionated explanation from children who customarily aren't very forthcoming, I've made peace with their impression of me.

Forget that you've seen the movie 18 times and know every line by heart. Forget that you know how it ends. Place yourself at the skill level of the students. Experiment with phrases that encourage smart guessing:

- I wonder...
- I don't know, this got pretty complicated.
- Sometimes it's hard to figure out.
- Hmmm, this is kind of confusing.
- I'm not sure, you could go several different ways here.
- Wow, there's a lot happening here.

In combination with intonation, such uncertainty can be very effective with all three groups of Mindreaders (Figures 6.2, 6.3, and 6.4).

Given a student's limited statement...	I mediate with uncertainty...	And the student continues...
1. Trixie wants to go back.	1. I wonder why...?	1. She wants to go back to the laundry place to get Knuffle Bunny back.
2. I dunno.	2. Yeah, I'm not sure either...	2. I know — he's gonna jump out.

Figure 6.2. Effective uncertainty with Junior Mindreaders

Given a student's limited statement...	I mediate with uncertainty...	And the student continues...
1. The boy went under the table.	1. That's kind of strange — I wonder why he did that.	1. He's gonna go look for his frog — he wants to find him and put him back in his pocket.
2. He's getting mad.	2 You think so...?	2. Yeah, he's mad because Tracy doesn't want to be around him.
3. She's wants to get it back.	3. Really?	3. Well, no, I guess she'll wait and see if he gets it.

Figure 6.3. Moving Up Mindreaders' responses to vague comments

Given a student's limited statement...	I mediate with uncertainty...	And the student continues...
1. Snape is taking Harry down to his room.	1. I wonder why...?	1. Because he's going to teach him about the brain invasion stuff.
2. Now he can't put scary guys in.	2. I wonder what his new plan will be...	2. Maybe he's gonna put the Indian in — like in the picture on the cover.
3. I don't know why he did that...	3. Yeah, this is kind of confusing...	3. Well, I guess he's gonna go back to his room and plan a way to get past that guard.

Figure 6.4. Varsity Mindreaders taking the lead

Encourage and guide students to watch a scene more than once before you offer additional mediation. Accept their partial answers, then cue them to information that may help them recognize additional details. Discuss this additional information prior to watching the scene again. You may find yourself replaying a scene four or five times. Watch as many times as you think would be helpful. Replaying doesn't mean you're doing a bad job of mediating; rather, it means you're guiding your actions based on your observations of the children in the given moment.

Focus on the Social Detective (Winner & Crooke, 2008) aspects of deciphering social situations. Appeal to the scientific leanings of students as you dig for contextual, verbal, and nonverbal information and the social consequences that follow. By making sure students know that unexpected events happen all the time, we can alleviate some of their uncertainty about a world that's constantly in social motion.

Quitting Time: That's a Wrap!

One important skill when using mediating tools is recognizing when they're no longer needed. You don't constantly have to be stretching out a student's language through your verbal mediation, just as you certainly don't have to use nonverbal aids when working with thoughts and feelings. In fact, you may not need to call upon these tools at all if tasks are moving along and reaching a level of language and interaction appropriate for those involved.

What you want the students to develop is the ability to figure out social interactions more quickly, and in real time. While it's true that these students will always struggle with social understanding, over time they'll gain more skills and strategies and feel more confident in their attempts to decipher the confusing world of social relationships. As soon as the sticky notes or emotions strips seem unnecessary during Movie Time work, stop using them and work at the more abstract level of "what is he thinking in his thought bubble" through discussion alone. Many children are unaccustomed to working at the high level of engagement required by the Movie Time program. Once they understand that they're required to put effort into the process, and they realize that you'll support them as needed, you may be surprised at how hard they work and how capable they are.

Young cat, if you keep your eyes open enough, oh, the stuff you would learn. The most wonderful stuff!

– **Dr. Seuss,** *I Can Read with My Eyes Shut*

Chapter 7

FIRST Lessons: Spy Eye Tasks

Spy Eye tasks focus on the most elemental — but still very complex — Social Thinking concepts. They provide an entry point for the more sophisticated social thought addressed in Detective Head and Me Too! tasks. Spy Eye tasks explore context and the thoughts, feelings, and plans of individual characters within the context. By using Spy Eye tasks, you encourage students to practice thinking with their eyes about what's going on around them and using basic perspective taking skills to read the minds of others.

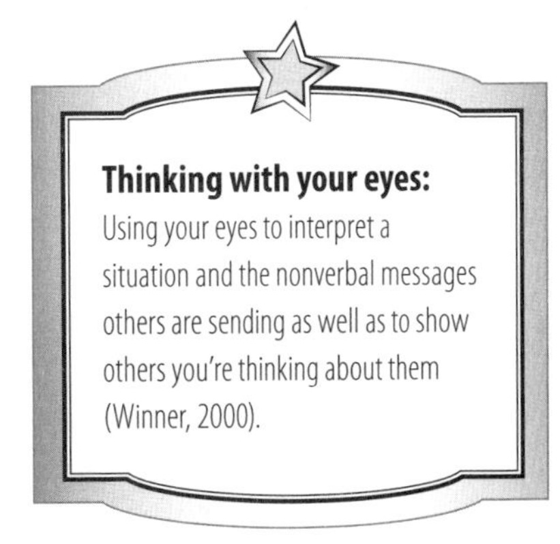

Thinking with your eyes: Using your eyes to interpret a situation and the nonverbal messages others are sending as well as to show others you're thinking about them (Winner, 2000).

These tasks work well with a wide range of Mindreaders, preschool through high school. Teachers who incorporate Movie Time Social Learning into a broader program to encourage better social thinking skills may need to remind students of the Social Thinking concepts and vocabulary mentioned below prior to talking about them in movie sessions. If Movie Time Social Learning is a stand-alone program, verify that students understand these basic concepts and have these emerging skills. If not, pre-teaching of the concepts and vocabulary should be done first. There's nothing worse than playing a movie scene and encouraging discussion only to be met with blank stares from students because there has been no prior teaching of Social Thinking beforehand.

For many children, these Spy Eye activities mark the first time they've thought and talked about movies with this kind of focus and depth. The social tasks in Spy Eye activities vary in complexity depending on the Mindreader level and include:

- Using contextual cues to identify the "where" and the "what's happening"
- Understanding visual gaze and referencing
- Reading a single character's basic body language (e.g., hands on hips when angry)
- Projecting what a single character is thinking, feeling, and what the character's next action might be
- Extrapolating feelings (e.g., happy, sad, mad/angry, afraid/scared, surprised)

This chapter describes the components of Spy Eye tasks for each Mindreader group and suggests strategies to use with each group.

The following are some examples of suggested discussion questions to use during Spy Eye tasks. They pertain to scenes in three movies, with each movie intended for a different group of Mindreader. (Chapters 8 and 9 include the suggested Detective Head and Me Too! discussion questions for each of these same scenes.) A full lesson plan for each of these movies is included on the CD. You can use these questions as a model as you prepare to show scenes from other movies to students.

Scene from *No Roses for Harry*

Spy Eye Questions for Junior Mindreaders

- What's Harry thinking and feeling when he hears Grandma is coming to visit?
- What's Harry thinking and feeling as the family searches for the sweater? What are the family members thinking and feeling?
- When you first see Grandma, do you notice something special about her?
- When Harry is barking and looking up in the tree, what's he looking at? How does he feel?
- How do the children and Grandma feel when they see the nest?
- How does Harry feel about the new sweater? Why?

Scene from *The Indian in the Cupboard*

Spy Eye Questions for Moving Up Mindreaders

- When he wakes up, what are Omri's thoughts, feelings, and plan as he walks toward the cabinet?
- When he's at school, how is Omri feeling? What's his plan?

Scene from *Harry Potter and the Order of the Phoenix*

Spy Eye Questions for Varsity Mindreaders

- Where is this? What is the setting here?

- What's the mood of the class before Umbridge comes in?
- What do we already know about Professor Umbridge?
- How does her cheerful disposition hide her true intentions?
- As she comes up the aisle, what are the students thinking?
- As the students look at their books, what are they thinking?
- Why does Umbridge laugh at the end of the scene — how is she feeling?

Spy Eye Tasks with Junior Mindreaders

Spy Eye questions are important but not always easy for this group. Expect that Junior Mindreaders will spend a lot of time on Spy Eye activities.

Importance of Language

Because Junior Mindreaders usually exhibit language delay, strive for detailed, clear language as you move through Spy Eye tasks with this group of children. One goal of these activities is to help students expand their language along with their social understanding.

Students respond to Movie Time Social Learning prompts for contextual information with answers that show a wide range in specificity—for example, if I ask "Who?" about a character, a child may answer "he," "man," or with more contextual information, "the dad." If I ask, "What's happening?," a child might just answer "cooking," "cooking soup," "The man is cooking," or a statement with more contextual information, such as "The dad is cooking dinner" or "The boy is waiting for the man to cook him dinner." More sophisticated linguistic form and syntax reflect deeper conceptual understanding. Encourage children to give more than a one-word answer. You can cue them to notice and respond to important details in the scene by pointing, tapping, or running your finger on the screen.

In the following example of a Spy Eye task, I worked with a student on creating social narrative around an unfamiliar scene. The use of silence and gesture was all seven-year-old Alexandra needed to substantially increase her language expression.

In *Pooh's Grand Adventure: The Search for Christopher Robin,* acorns are starting to rain down and make a big pile that will ultimately pick up the characters and carry them down the road. I stopped the video on a wide shot of characters with the acorns coming down on them and started with an open-ended question to establish context.

Anna: What's happening?

Alexandra: The acorns get big... (*looking confused*)

Anna: But the acorns are still small... (*I look somewhat confused and gesture to indicate a small size.*)

Alexandra: The acorns, the acorns ... they gonna ... gonna... (*looks confused, starts gesturing: pointing, moving arm up, shaking wrist like the falling acorns*) All the acorns ... down... (*gesturing down, gesturing up and down with hands, turning palms down*) The acorns, all the acorns falling down and there's, there's gonna be a pile. (*gestures big pile, pauses, looking at the frozen image on the screen*)

Anna: (*nodding*)

Alexandra: They're gonna fall in a big, big pile, and they go on Winnie the Pooh and everybody — it's so funny! (*Alexandra seems very pleased with herself, as if I was the one who had been confused.*)

By allowing Alexandra to work through this process, which took two to three minutes, she came up with her own original thought. Her final language came out easily and smoothly compared to her initial description, reflecting how far she'd come in complexity of thought and language. When her mother came to pick her up, we replayed the scene and Alexandra described it again, labeling it her "favorite."

Exploring Context with Junior Mindreaders

Spy Eye tasks begin with identifying the "where" of a social event. Mindreaders of all levels, but especially Junior Mindreaders, often focus on irrelevant details in identifying context. Identifying the "where" involves:

- Scanning environments quickly
- Sorting relevant from irrelevant details

- Thinking about their own experiences to make generalizations about context (e.g., "That kinda looks like the place I shop with Mom — I guess it's a store.")
- Making semantic judgments about characters (e.g., "Is that a mom or a teacher?")

While these steps seem easy and logical to most neurotypical people, they're difficult for children with social cognitive challenges, many of whom are detail thinkers. Often you'll need to begin by asking the students to identify a more accurate understanding of the "where." It may be necessary to use gestures and point to important aspects of the scene slowly, allowing childrens' understanding to develop over time. When children focus on irrelevant information or are imprecise in determining context, you can use several strategies, including the following:

- Deconstruct why the answer isn't a "smart guess." Probe for more information about why they answered as they did, which will give you a sense of what personal experiences and memories they used as a basis for their opinion. Try to understand why they've made the error, and move them forward from that point. Let them know you understand (at least somewhat) why they made the choices they did.
- Stress what was correct about the answer, compliment them for coming up with an answer, and work together to identify what another answer might be.
- Try using additional or different mediating tools, as described in Chapters 4, 5, and 6. Pointing can be an effective prompt to cue visual attention.

Figuring out the setting is crucial to determining what's expected of the characters in that situation. With Spy Eye tasks, you challenge Junior Mindreaders to explore new degrees of flexibility and generalization as they identify where the characters are and what they're doing there. To do this, they need to think with their eyes, use their social memory to incorporate their own world knowledge and then expand on it to include similar but different experiences.

For example, if a movie shows part of a living room that includes a staircase going up and shag carpeting everywhere, viewers need to draw on their general experiences of living rooms to recognize the one in the movie for what it is, even if they've never seen a living room exactly like it.

For neurotypical brains, the formula (front door + couch + tables + lamps = living room) is easily recognized. For children with social learning limitations, however, these generalizations can be difficult to make and require sufficient processing time. They struggle with seeing the big picture and forming a concept (a living room) from those details (central coherence challenges). Their initial response is often marked by confusion: "How is *that* a living room? *I've* never been in a house that looks like *that* … ." It becomes a living room only when they generalize the commonalities with other living rooms. Your goal is to help them develop the fundamental social thinking skills from which generalization will arise and improve. Be patient; this type of social learning doesn't happen overnight and often requires lots of practice.

Correctly identifying context is key to understanding whatever social interaction takes place in a scene. For example, in the movie *Frog Goes to Dinner*, if the children don't correctly interpret that the boy and his parents are returning home, their understanding of the entire scene will be limited. Note the difference between the following two statements:

"They are coming *in* [the door]."
"The *family* is coming *home*."

While both statements are true, only the second one gives a sense of event. By specifying that the context is home, "they" becomes a family returning — a unit, rather than random individuals — and the children can interpret upcoming events based on the concept of family.

The makeup of a scene — the individuals (the "who") and the environment in which they find themselves (the "where") — lays the foundation for the action (the "what") that transpires. Spy Eye tasks slow down the action to allow careful processing of contextual information to take place so students can then make sense of what occurs in the relationships.

Jump Cuts: Complicating Context

We all frequently enter a situation where others are already interacting and we don't know what has already occurred. Or, during an interaction, we may turn away for a few minutes, missing some of what's been done or said. We need to use efficient social processing to understand what's gone on and act appropriately.

Movies allow many opportunities to practice this type of processing, with rapid "jump cuts" within a scene or from one scene to the next that delete obvious information. "One second your character is just sitting down; the next second he's seated, with a cup of coffee in his hand. … The viewer doesn't actually need to *see* the man finish sitting down, pour himself a cup of coffee, stir in sugar, then start sipping it. You can jump right from sitting to sipping, and the viewer's brain will fill the rest in" (Snider, 2010).

Junior Mindreaders aren't able to easily or speedily fill in gaps and moments they miss, whether in their everyday lives or on the screen. When children seem confused by a jump cut, it's usually about sequencing events and identifying missing information. If children have difficulty with jump cuts in Spy Eye activities, you can:

- Go back to the previous scene to ascertain where the action was taking place
- Check previous scenes for a quick set of transitional frames that may pass rapidly but show the context changing (e.g., a quick shutting of a car door as the character arrives at a new location is meant to communicate that he's gone somewhere new)
- Contrast the "where" of the previous and current scenes using sketching or writing as visual supports
- Work with the students to note differences in contextual details (Is the furniture the same? Which characters are present?)
- Encourage the students to play a "spot the scene change" game, challenging them to notice when the action shifts to a different location

Thoughts and Feelings Lead to Action

In Spy Eye activities, you take Junior Mindreaders through a step-by-step understanding of how characters in movie scenes experience feelings based on where they are and what's happening, form opinions based on those feelings, and then translate those thoughts and opinions into plans. This process is at the core of Spy Eye tasks.

Once children have identified context, they begin to consider the thoughts, feelings, and ultimately, the actions of the characters. They note where the characters are looking and figure out what's being communicated by their facial expressions, body language, and words. You'll want to:

- Help children focus on who the characters are, what object or person the characters are thinking about, what the characters are thinking about that object or person, and how the characters might be feeling
- Expand how children identify and talk about feelings
- Help develop children's ability to remember and access their prior knowledge of the characters
- Support children in figuring out what the character's next action might be

As you work on Spy Eye tasks to identify thoughts, feelings, and plans with Junior Mindreaders, remember to use visual aids. For children with only a developing ability to identify emotions in others, the ability to point to a correct feeling picture is progress. With younger children, you may need to start with happy, sad, angry, and okay and then add afraid

and excited when appropriate. Combining multiple visual supports works well with Junior Mindreaders, such as creating both simple sketches of characters' expressions and thought bubbles to show differing perspectives and feelings of characters.

When the students identify thoughts and feelings, some may first relate a character's thought while others will first talk about the character's feeling. In teaching social thinking, we help students appreciate that everyone has thoughts and feelings, and that thoughts and feelings are connected to what's happening around them. What the children give you may not be exactly in this order or what you're looking for, but it's still information you can work with. The following table shows the type of statements Junior Mindreaders might make to describe characters' thoughts and feelings during Spy Eye activities and possible strategies you can use.

	A student might say...	Your prompt might be to...
Student expresses the feeling first	"He's mad."	1. Draw a feeling bubble. 2. Point to the object or event causing the feeling. 3. Say "Maybe he's mad because..." 4. Say "I wonder why he's mad?"
Student expresses the thought first	"He wants the cookie."	1. Draw a thought bubble. 2. Point to the character's expression. 3. Offer picture choices of feelings (such as emotions strips). 4. Say "He wants the cookie, so maybe he's feeling..." 5. Say "It looks like he's feeling..."

Figure 7.1. Possible options to expand statements by Junior Mindreaders

Helping children build connections between thoughts and feelings can be challenging. In the example below, I worked to mediate a thought bubble with a Junior Mindreader while watching *Sylvester and the Magic Pebble.* I went in circles for a bit using open-ended questions before I switched the type of prompt. Once I found the right prompt for the child in that *moment*, the answer wasn't hard to elicit.

Anna: Let's think of a thought bubble for Sylvester's mom and dad. What's your idea?

Eli: They are sad.

Anna: I think so, too; that's how they are feeling. What are they thinking?

Eli: They are looking out the window.

Anna: Well, that's what they are doing. What are they thinking?

Eli: They are sad.

Anna: You think they are feeling sad. They are feeling sad because... *(This proved to be an effective strategy.)*

Eli: Because Sylvester is lost.

You may find that Junior Mindreaders can identify what a character is thinking about but are unable to take the next step to accurately discern a character's opinions or plans. It's a big leap in social processing, and understandable! For example, a child might say "a dog is thinking about a sweater" yet be unable to say more. When that happens, you can choose from these strategies:

- Watch the scene again.
- Use more visuals.
- Review what you know about the character.
- Involve the children in acting out the scene.
- Move on!

Some children will "get" more of the movie than others. You're looking for improved understanding, not immediate and total comprehension. Recognizing and verbalizing a thought is a challenging task. If you ask a young child with social cognitive challenges to share his thoughts on a given subject, you'll often get no response or "I don't know." Yet sharing thoughts is what allows people to have conversations using a Social Thinking strategy known as "add a thought" (Winner, 2002).

If I say, "That coffee smells great" and you say, "Mmm, sure does," our individual thoughts about the coffee initiated our statements, which we then shared with each other. That exchange is how we come to know that we have pretty much the same opinion about the coffee. Children with social learning challenges have trouble developing this ability.

Plan is a difficult concept that hinges on several variables: the character's thoughts, the context of the setting, what has happened in the scene up to that point, and the influence other people in the scene — with their own thoughts and feelings — exert. It's much easier for children to identify what someone might be thinking about than it is to recognize what the character wants to do next. I've struggled many times to help a child get to that level of understanding.

Some plans are obvious and easy to figure out when they relate to personal experiences, such as "I'm thinking about the cookie — I want to eat it." Or "It's raining — I'm thinking about going inside or getting my umbrella." Plans involving an opinion are more difficult; for example, "I like my frog — I'm going to take it to the restaurant with me" or "I don't like spinach — I'm not going to eat my serving."

To help Junior Mindreaders begin to talk about identifying a plan in a Spy Eye activity, you can try the following strategies:

- Use different words. (For example: What does the character want to do with X? What will he do now or next? What is he thinking about X?)
- Work with the concept of "like versus don't like." Children with social learning deficits have difficulties forming opinions. The game Whoonu (Cranium Games) has a large number of cards listing objects and experiences children can practice sorting for themselves (e.g., "I like pancakes but I don't like hot tubs").
- Use visuals to elicit *details* about a plan. Draw descriptive pictures or write down any words the children say to expand the thought. (For example, if a child says "baseball... get baseball ... wants it," you could write that down and add the prompt "because..." to elicit a detailed plan: "The girl wants the baseball because she likes it.")

Remember that following the social thoughts of a character is a difficult task. You'll want to support this complicated thinking in as many concrete ways as you can to help you and the students stay on track.

Whenever possible, encourage the children to verbalize the specific reason for a plan but accept a simplified plan if that's all they currently are able to formulate ("He's gonna eat the cookie").

As you discuss feelings with Junior Mindreaders in Spy Eye tasks, keep in mind that "okay" is a feeling. In our efforts to teach about feelings to children with social learning difficulties, we may sometimes stress what we consider to be "real" feeling words, such as happy or afraid, even though often during the day *we* feel "just okay" instead of happy, sad, frustrated, or angry. Exposing children to the label for that neutral feeling zone is as important as teaching them to distinguish between emotions such as annoyed and furious.

Remember that helping children build connections between thoughts and feelings can be challenging work. Many of these tasks are harder than you might expect.

Spy Eye Tasks with Moving Up Mindreaders

Many of the simpler Spy Eye tasks aren't terribly difficult for Moving Up Mindreaders; they have relatively strong competencies in establishing context and reading minds when situations aren't overly complex or out of their comfort range. However, they can still find it difficult to identify a context out of their own experiences, recognize the "why" behind a character's specific thought or plan, or identify a more complicated feeling state.

Language and Moving Up Mindreaders

As they work through Spy Eye tasks, Moving Up Mindreaders will continue to develop their social thinking and perspective taking skills to use them more fluidly and without as much processing time. As they become better social thinkers, their language skills will also improve — with your help, of course — especially their abilities to formulate complex sentences and to express a clear narrative by linking complex sentences together in logical ways. Many things happen in the movies they watch, and often relatively quickly. Unlike the language skills expected of Junior Mindreaders, Moving Up Mindreaders can be prompted and taught to use more than simple sentences to describe context.

For example, as he viewed *The Pink Panther*, William worked hard to describe a scene. He had some trouble getting going with his language formation, although this was a very good start and demonstrates his emerging sequencing skills: "At first they were cheering with the anticipation of the game, but when they saw the kiss, *suddenly* and their attention was changed *suddenly* ... Do you not disagree?" William's rising intonation on the last "suddenly" indicated that he hadn't finished his thought. If his intonation had fallen, he actually would have had a good explanation, albeit one that omitted information about the new object of their attention. In this case, further mediating strategies, such as sketching out the sequence he was struggling to explain or writing out his language so he could keep track of where he was going verbally, could have helped him formulate a more complete explanation.

As students develop a more nuanced level of social thinking, their need for more complex language grows with it. Consider an event from *Like Mike,* a movie suggested for

Moving Up Mindreaders. The movie features Tracy, a professional basketball player, and his friend Calvin, a young orphan whose newly acquired magical shoes have allowed him to be on a professional team. Tracy jokingly tells Calvin not to put paint on the window, but Calvin does (he can tell Tracy won't really mind). Most Moving Up Mindreaders are still developing their ability to use some of the complex social thinking required to accurately interpret this scene: understanding context, picking out relevant visual cues, understanding friendly humor, and interpreting motives and intent. Those who are actively becoming more proficient in using these social thinking skills will want more complex language to explain their ideas. As mediator, you can recognize and capitalize on these advanced learning opportunities! The tasks in Movie Time Social Learning provide rich yet structured opportunities to work on language skills that go hand-in-hand with expanding social thinking.

Exploring Context with Moving Up Mindreaders

Moving Up Mindreaders work with movies that are set in a wide range of places. In the two Moving Up Mindreader movies presented in this book, contexts include: on an airplane, at a hotel, at a pharmacy, in a school hallway, on a busy urban street, and at a skateboard park. Before embarking on identifying thoughts and feelings of characters, it's wise to take a moment to confirm that the correct context has been identified. After all, the judgments Moving Up Mindreaders will be making in Spy Eye (and Detective Head) tasks hinge on knowing where the action is taking place and what behaviors might be expected there.

As with Junior Mindreaders, Moving Up Mindreaders can find jump cuts challenging, with transitions between contexts marked with very fleeting images. (See the discussion in "Jump Cuts: Complicating Context" earlier in this chapter for addressing difficulties in processing jump cuts.) Such jump cuts remind us that, although a shot may not contain characters, it nevertheless gives us important information about the characters and is worthy of notice. If children don't process these cuts, it will be difficult to make sense of what follows. You may want to review the shift in context by watching it several times slowly, talking them through the cut, or even taking photos of the two contexts so you can discuss them side by side.

Exploring Thoughts, Feelings, and Plans

Once they've identified the context, students can consider the expected behaviors in that situation as they work to identify the thoughts of multiple characters at the same time. What makes viewers laugh in *Like Mike* when Calvin races around the hotel room like a tornado is that we understand that is unexpected behavior in a hotel. Shared knowledge of expected and unexpected behavior is often what supports the "why" behind thoughts.

In Spy Eye activities, Moving Up Mindreaders are asked to identify the thoughts of multiple characters at the same time. Especially when students are new to Movie Time Social Learning, it's best to slow down your pace, break a scene into discrete character elements, use silence to give students time to think about the various characters and their thoughts, write things down, and speak slowly with plenty of pauses.

Moving Up Mindreaders have a lot to think about and can process information slowly. As they work on identifying the feelings of characters and the reasons behind those feelings, Moving Up Mindreaders are exposed to new emotional territory. For these students, it's important to work on:

- Broadening their ability to talk about feelings in general
- Exposing them to more finely tuned emotional labels ("annoyed" instead of just "mad")
- Attending carefully to why an emotional reaction takes place
- Preparing them to juggle different emotional reactions by different characters to the same event (required in Detective Head tasks discussed in the next chapter)

Many of the same tools used for context identification — especially working slowly and providing a lot of silent time for processing — will be useful here.

In the movies discussed in this book, Moving Up Mindreaders learn that words don't always communicate the actual truth — sometimes true intent is revealed through tone, facial expression, or even by what is *not* said. Characters begin to give "mixed messages," which need to be sorted out.

In the example below, William tried to make sense of such a discrepancy in a scene from *The Pink Panther.* He realized his initial answer wasn't correct and almost gave up but then suddenly came up with a smart guess that used more of the information on screen and gave interesting information about the Chief Inspector character. William's answer also shows how his social thinking was moving forward, especially when he had time to think. At the end William used a conjunction ('cuz) that shows he finally made the connection between the smile and the feeling state it reflects.

Anna: The Chief Inspector has been nominated seven times, and he's never won. How is he feeling about that? (*an open-ended question*)

William: Very sad.

Anna: He is saying "I have never won," but he's smiling. Why is he smiling?

William: He's amazed. He sounds amazed.

Anna: But why is he *smiling*? (*emphatic intonation*)

William: Um, uh, um, he's trying to tell us that it's really funny.

Anna: Is it funny?

William: No. No, it's not funny. I don't know. I absolutely don't know. (*six-second pause*) 'Cuz he's embarrassed.

Spy Eye Tasks with Varsity Mindreaders: Checking Fundamental Skills

Compared with Junior Mindreaders, Varsity Mindreaders are far ahead in their abilities to identify thoughts, feelings, and plans. However, they still need to review at least some Spy Eye activities. Don't make assumptions about what Varsity Mindreaders "obviously" understand.

Language Skills

The language of Varsity Mindreaders is more developed than that of the other two groups, although completeness and attention to personal relationships often are still issues. With Spy Eye tasks, your focus will be on checking basic social understanding before moving on to clear and complete language. Writing out the narrative (for example, as a paragraph on the dry-erase board) will allow children to add new and important thoughts (as phrases). Keeping track of ideas can be tricky because the students may go down a dead-end thought path and need to start over, make self-corrections by rephrasing, or expand narrative given the opportunity to read over what they've already formulated.

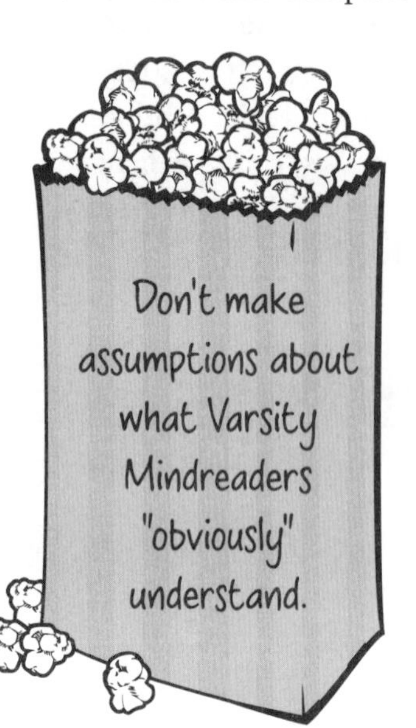

Although they've qualified to be Varsity Mindreaders, these students still have social learning limitations. Many of them rarely speak with the complexity you hear after you mediate their explanations. However, all of the tasks in Movie Time Social Learning give them chances to formulate a chunk of language and be successful at explaining their social perceptions.

Context Shifts

Although many Varsity Mindreaders can keep up with context shifts, don't assume that they're competent in this skill until you've checked several times. In the next example of a Spy Eye activity with a Varsity Mindreader, Eli was asked to identify a scene in *The Pink Panther,* but he didn't notice critical contextual information.

Clouseau has been dropped off by his partner on a residential street. He walks up to the front door to the building, unlocks it, and goes up the stairs to his apartment. Clouseau is on the landing in front of the door, which is ajar. He's suspicious that someone has broken in and is checking for his spare key. Eli responded: "He's at the police headquarters. I think he's sneaking into the Chief Inspector's office."

Eli totally missed the contextual information in the jump cut that told him Inspector Clouseau had arrived at the building where he lives. While the front door in the movie is similar to one you might see at a police station, Clouseau's approach, the appearance of the building and staircase, and the fact he's looking for a key all provide crucial information to determine his location. Because Eli missed this information, he lacked information needed to understand the next scene.

While some Varsity Mindreaders won't have to spend much time on fundamental Spy Eye tasks such as basic context shifts, others like Eli need practice noticing and making social sense of the information in movie scenes when the group is moving along at a quicker pace. If you find children need practice keeping up with rapid scene cuts, you may want to:

- Review the previous scene and establish accurate context
- Work to establish whatever "hints" were provided of the change, no matter how fleeting (such as the quick shot of Clouseau and his partner in the car on the street)
- Review the new scene shots, with careful examination of details to identify differences from the previous context

Thoughts, Feelings, and Plans

Like Moving Up Mindreaders, Varsity Mindreaders are asked to think about the thoughts, feelings, and plans of multiple characters. Plans may be formulated, played out, and perhaps revised as the movie progresses. While much of the work on thoughts, feelings, and plans is done at the more socially complex Detective Head level (the tasks focusing on how characters influence each other), Spy Eye tasks provide opportunities for Varsity Mindreaders to check their foundation of social understanding.

In the next example, a student re-evaluates his initial answer and proposes a second, accurate explanation about the "why" behind a discrete behavior — the Minister in *Harry*

Potter rapidly inhaling because he's shocked at what he sees. Initially, Tucker admitted he hadn't noticed it at all. More important, once it's pointed out, he struggled to make sense of the action and mistakenly indicated he thought the Minister had blown out rather than inhaled. Explaining the Minister's quick intake of air, just a split-second shot, provided information as to what the character is thinking and feeling. (I used restating and an open-ended question as strategies here.)

Anna: Now, initially you thought that maybe the Minister did something with air to get rid of Voldemort. What do you think about that now?

Tucker: I don't think that was right. I know that wasn't right. I think he was gasping because all of a sudden Voldemort is standing there and there's a dead kid on the ground and he thought Voldemort was gone. He can't believe it. He's dumbfounded. He's gonna realize he was wrong the whole movie.

This example shows how discrete behaviors can reveal important information. Varsity Mindreaders are asked to make sense of mixed messages — times when words and nonverbal information don't match but accurate understanding of the real message is vital. Breaking down behavior can be helpful in understanding the true intent of characters as well as of people in real life. Here are some suggested ways to break down behavior, considering a range of possibilities and focusing on using information that's already known:

- Write down both the verbal and nonverbal behavior.
- Identify the feelings that go with each type of behavior.
- Review previous knowledge about the character (including plan and motive).
- Focus on figuring out what the character is *really* thinking (sometimes this means generating more than one thought).
- Look critically at the possible answers.
- Choose which answer is probably correct given all of what's known.

Whether you're working with Junior Mindreaders, Moving Up Mindreaders, or Varsity Mindreaders, Spy Eye tasks will establish the social foundation needed to explore what happens when these characters interact. Once students have developed a familiarity and facility with identifying a single character's feelings, thoughts, and predicted next actions, they're ready to look at how the feelings, thoughts, and plans of multiple characters make the social story much more complex. They'll then be ready to branch out to Detective Head activities.

Every one of us is a Social Detective.
We are good Social Detectives when we use our eyes, ears, and brains to figure out what others are planning to do next or are presently doing and what they mean by their words and deeds.

– **Michelle Garcia Winner and Pamela Crooke,** *You Are a Social Detective!*

Chapter 8

MORE Complex Thought

Detective Head Tasks

Detective Head tasks, which build on Spy Eye skills, promote the understanding of more complex social relationships and social subtleties. In Spy Eye tasks, students begin to use different social thinking skills. As they develop their ability to think with their eyes and use basic perspective taking — to understand and explain what each character is doing, thinking, and feeling in a particular scene in a basic way — they're gaining the social thinking skills that help them move into considering relationships between characters on a more nuanced level. The social tasks in Detective Head include:

- More skillful identification of the perspectives, plans, and motives of multiple characters
- Studying how relationships develop over time
- Differentiating feelings on a more nuanced level, using more precise vocabulary
- Keeping up with quick changes in feelings within the same scene
- Processing subtleties of communication, including tone of voice, indirectness, and truth versus lies
- Forming opinions about the actions of characters

From Thoughts About One to Thoughts About Many

At the core of all Detective Head tasks is perspective taking. As a movie's story line evolves, various characters, along with the viewer, become aware of certain information. Others do not. Based on that information or lack of it, these characters think, act, plan, and react differently.

Differences in knowledge inform perspective. For example, in *Sylvester and the Magic Pebble,* viewers know the mother is sitting on Sylvester, but she thinks he's just a rock. Often what makes a story interesting is the process by which characters gather information and how that information changes their experience. Perspective is also about differences in interpretation and opinion. In *The Red Balloon,* even though one trolley conductor may think balloons don't belong on board, another may have no problem with the same scenario.

Even more than Spy Eye tasks, Detective Head tasks challenge all types of Mindreaders to work on strengthening their language skills to be able to express the complex ideas they're working on. While Spy Eye tasks focus on the thoughts and feelings of individuals, with Detective Head tasks students are asked to compare and contrast the thoughts and feelings of more than one person. Don't underestimate the power of visual aids as tools to support students' processing of multiple characters' opinions and plans. Remember, this is complicated social thinking; supports, patience, and practice are essential.

The following are examples of discussion questions to use during Detective Head tasks. They pertain to the same scenes in the movies presented at the beginning of the previous chapter for Spy Eye tasks. A full lesson plan for each of these movies is included on the CD. You can use these questions as a model as you prepare to show scenes from other movies to students.

Scene from *No Roses for Harry*

Detective Head Questions for Junior Mindreaders

- Why is the family looking for the sweater? Why can't anyone find it?
- Why does Harry want to go for a walk? What might his plan be? Does he know something the others don't?
- Does Grandma know how the bird got the wool from the sweater? Who does know?
- Why didn't Grandma send him another sweater with roses?

Scene from *The Indian in the Cupboard*

Detective Head Questions for Moving Up Mindreaders

- Track Omri's many changes in feelings: when opening the cabinet, when he thinks the cabinet is empty, when he sees the Indian, when he tries to touch the Indian, when the Indian stabs him, when he's talking to the Indian, and when his dad comes in.

- How is the Indian feeling? Why is he feeling that way and calling Omri "demon" and "giant"? Why does this confuse Omri?
- Even though the Indian isn't speaking English, can you tell what he's saying?
- Do you think it's a good idea to try to touch someone who has a knife, even if the person is very small? What else might Omri have done?
- Why didn't Omri show his dad the Indian — what do you think his dad would have done?
- As they walk to school, why does Omri's mom ask him if he forgot something at home?

Scene from *Harry Potter and the Order of the Phoenix*

Detective Head Questions for Varsity Mindreaders

- Why do Harry and Ron smile when Umbridge comes to the head of the class and mentions O.W.L.s?
- Ron speaks out without being reprimanded. When Harry speaks out, why does Umbridge respond so harshly? Did the tone of Harry's voice have anything to do with it?
- What do you think about Umbridge's statement that doing well on tests is what school is all about?
- How does everyone react to Harry's mention of Voldemort's name?
- How do Harry's and Umbridge's feelings escalate during their disagreement?

Detective Head Tasks for Junior Mindreaders

Once Junior Mindreaders can identify the thoughts, feelings, and plans of individual characters in Spy Eye tasks, they move on to Detective Head tasks and practice putting these ideas together and examining contrasting perspectives. Detective Head tasks for Junior Mindreaders consist of:

- Untangling multiple perspectives
- Explaining characters' opinions of objects, events, and other characters (to the degree that a viewer can express someone else's thoughts)
- Generating their own opinions about choices the characters make
- Identifying the thoughts and actions of characters, taking into consideration the actions and feelings of other characters
- Continuing to identify feeling states
- Discussing how characters influence each other

Junior Mindreaders are beginning to understand the complexities behind perspective taking but usually can't manipulate the concepts sufficiently to make a smart guess without the use of visual aids. For example, as shown in Figure 8.1, a child who was able to state the plans of the two characters in *Knuffle Bunny* didn't understand that these plans conflicted with each other until I drew arrows to clarify the concept.

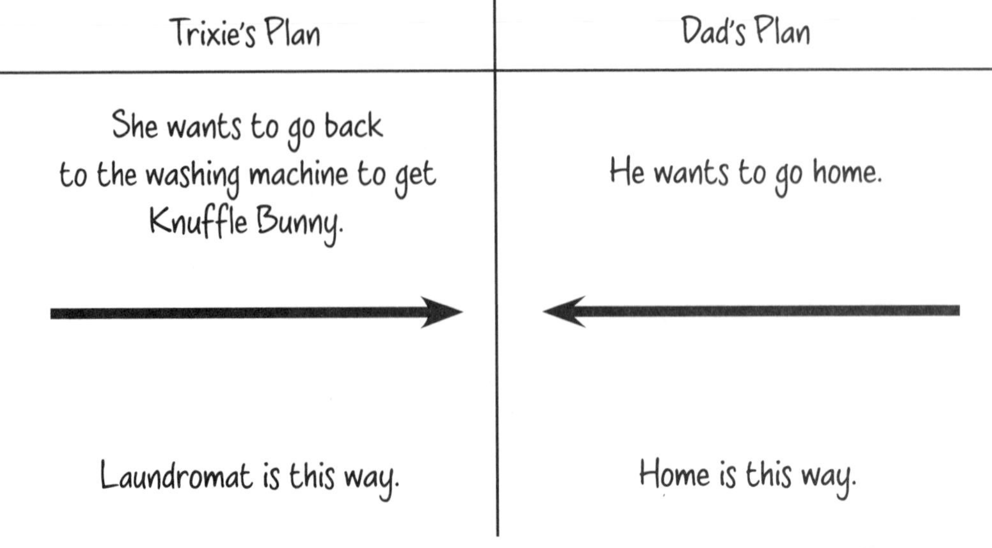

Figure 8.1. Visual aid to support a Junior Mindreader's understanding of perspective (*Knuffle Bunny*)

Students who can identify one person's thoughts in isolated statements can become quite confused when asked to consider divergent perspectives concurrently. If one viewer likes the sweater with roses in *No Roses for Harry*, her perspective may make it difficult for her to recognize that Harry doesn't like it. When the students' own perspectives interfere with understanding how characters may feel in a scene, you can incorporate this occurrence into your work instead of ignore it. Ways to do this include:

- Helping students recognize they're having a thought about something on the screen
- Creating a visual to represent each student
- Encouraging the students to insert themselves as characters and add their own thought bubbles to those of the onscreen characters

Though Junior Mindreaders working on Detective Head tasks grapple with divergent opinions, differences in perspective are key to the unfolding story because characters' opinions determine their plans. Junior Mindreaders are making progress even if they're only able to sort preprinted thought bubbles on sticky notes that state different opinions among characters. Over time, they'll be able to generate thought bubbles for the characters on their own.

Perspective taking as a whole may be troublesome for many of your students. Children may struggle to understand that people have thoughts and opinions that differ from their own and then struggle even more trying to "put themselves in someone else's shoes." Because the perspective taking tasks in Detective Head can be extremely challenging, you may want to provide young children with additional teaching related to perspective taking outside the venue of movie watching. A few suggestions include:

- Pretending with objects (for example, "This is a basket, but I'm pretending it's a hat.")
- Placing surprising objects in containers with packaging that leads to assumptions about what's inside, such as crackers in a box of crayons ("What will another child think is in there?")
- Playing games by moving objects to confuse returning visitors (for example, "Janey thinks the puzzle is in the basket, but when she was out of the room we moved it!")

Particularly with Junior Mindreaders who are relatively new to the concept of perspective, it's helpful to make the learning fun with the use of humor. In *Frog Goes to Dinner*, the fact that we know the frog is in the saxophone, but the saxophonist who is about to play it doesn't, can get an entire group of children covering their mouths giggling. In such amusing interactions, the foundations of perspective taking are laid.

Detective Head tasks can be a big step up from Spy Eye tasks as students are asked, perhaps for the first time, to identify and give an opinion about someone else's plan. However, even children with language formulation issues can work through these tasks if you have a diverse set of visual and verbal mediating tools. Visual supports, such as drawings, thought bubbles, and written narrative, which can all be used in combination, will assist children in keeping information straight while they consider "What do *you* think that person is planning to do?"

Junior Mindreaders also will be asked to continue to think carefully about feelings of characters. In Detective Head tasks, characters' feelings may change more rapidly than in Spy Eye tasks. More important, the feelings of characters influence each other. With the help of mediating tools, children can work on constructing more complex language to explain these connections as they practice inserting "because" into their statements about thoughts and feelings.

When you find yourself stuck on a particular point (and you will!), you can move on. If you feel everyone is becoming confused, make a change and come back to the work later. Make a mental note of what type of task was "too much," and focus on it using an easier example in the future. You're teaching difficult, abstract concepts to generally rigid thinkers with limited knowledge and experience. When you don't achieve your initial goal, don't feel you've "wasted" the session. Understanding these complex ideas requires assimilation and accommodations; success isn't usually achieved in a half hour. Repeated sessions may be necessary depending on the perspective taking abilities of your students.

Moving Up Mindreaders: Upping the Ante

Moving Up Mindreaders spend much of their time with Movie Time Social Learning working on Detective Head tasks. They'll be challenged by tasks when they're asked to:

- Identify and monitor multiple perspectives concurrently.
- Track opinions and plans of multiple characters.
- Understand the reasons for rapid shifts in feelings.

The movies you'll screen for Moving Up Mindreaders are substantially different from those used with Junior Mindreaders in that they:

- Are live action rather than animated
- Portray characters with greater depth
- Show more complex relationships between characters
- Develop scenes more rapidly
- Include more nuances
- Have more mature themes

Your job is to slow things down, rewind scenes, and offer enough support to help students learn to catch those shifts and differences and understand the "why" behind them.

It's important not to make assumptions about the skills of the students, as demonstrated in the next interchange, when I watched *The Indian in the Cupboard* with an eleven-year-old Moving Up Mindreader. I asked what I thought was going to be an easy question about perspective and motive translating to action. The surprise was on me!

Choosing one scene and discussing it in depth can be more productive than speeding through two or three scenes.

In the scene, Omri, the main character, is walking to school with a fanny pack that holds a toy Indian and a cowboy who magically have been made real. He's walking *very* slowly and carefully, even though he's late for school. He knows his friend Patrick will be eager to see them (he's in on the secret). Patrick is waiting for Omri at the school gate, but the bell rings and the teacher makes him go inside. The freeze-frame shows Omri walking down the street slowly and looking down at the fanny pack. Note that I used open-ended questions, silence, and facial expressions as mediating strategies here.

Anna: Why is Omri walking so slowly?

Justin: So Patrick won't see him ... (Answer is given very quickly — it's true, Patrick didn't see him because he had already gone inside. Justin may be using the conjunction "so" or past tense incorrectly.)

Anna: (*I follow his idea instead of correcting him.*) Why doesn't he want Patrick to see him?

Justin: No, that's not it ... (*looking confused*)

Anna: (*six-second pause*) Think again, why is Omri walking so slowly?

Justin: He doesn't want to go to school?

Anna: Hmmm. Think about what you know about Omri going to school that day.

Justin: (*five-second pause; looks away but is clearly thinking*) Oh, yeah! (*sits up, reconnects with me, eyes brighten animatedly, index finger goes up in an "aha" gesture*) He's bringing them to school to show Patrick. He knows Patrick really wants to see them but he doesn't want to jiggle them so he has to walk slowly! (*Notice the complexity of this explanation.*) That's why he's late. (*additional extrapolation from contextual clues of the yard being empty and the bell having rung*) I get it! (*clear change in Justin's affect to seeming quite pleased to have made sense of this small detail*)

Anna: (*rewinding DVD, smiling and nodding*) It sounds like you're figuring it out. Let's watch again and check what you think. (We replayed it so Justin could confirm he had come to a good conclusion and to see the short scene again with this new realization. As we watch this time, Justin smiles and nods as the scene unfolds.)

With Detective Head tasks, Moving Up Mindreaders are challenged to decipher multiple and varying plans, motives, and feelings. Choosing one scene and discussing it in depth can be more productive than speeding through two or three scenes. Students who have already seen the movie may be impatient to get to a part they liked (one you may not be showing because limited social interaction takes place). Typically their impatience marks their lack of complete understanding and desire to gloss over the details. They *think* they get it but they really only get part of it (usually the obvious), just as in real life. It's in getting the rest of it through slow, careful viewing that they learn crucial social concepts to apply in the real world.

Eliciting Opinions

You can use Detective Head tasks to test students' understanding of a scene by asking what *they* think about a character's plan. Forming an opinion involves perspective taking, judgment, and flexible (rather than black-and-white) thinking.

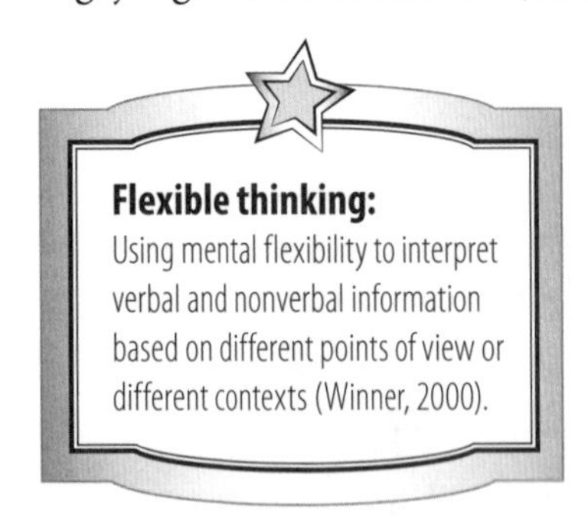

Though they can generate such personal opinions more easily than Junior Mindreaders, Moving Up Mindreaders can still find doing so a challenge. You can encourage them by starting with "thumbs up" or "thumbs down" responses, writing or drawing a specific character's plan on a dry-erase board, or mediating their language to support what they're trying to express.

While Spy Eye tasks target identification of emotions in a relatively narrow, one-character-at-a-time fashion, tracking changes in feelings within one or more characters in Detective Head tasks helps Moving Up Mindreaders understand the fluidity of emotions. In Detective Head tasks, tracking these emotions can be helped by:

- Providing lists of feelings for students to use
- Tracking the transitions within the scene that move along the action (and the feelings)
- Writing down feelings as the group generates them
- Analyzing a feeling for its intensity, when appropriate

In Figure 8.2, a short, three-minute scene provides a rich example of how quickly feelings arise and change and how those feelings relate closely to how another person is feeling and what's happening. We identified each event in the scene and watched it at least three times, with an emphasis on identifying how each character felt during each event. Although this particular group was able to discuss why Omri and Patrick were feeling the way they were without any other supporting visuals, another group might need to lay out the information in a different way.

This is what our final chart looked like:

Scene: Omri and Patrick at School (*The Indian in the Cupboard*)

Event 1. Patrick wanted to show the boys Boone and Little Bear.

Omri: Scared, freaked out
Patrick: Excited, happy

Event 2. Omri stopped Patrick. They argue.

Omri: Upset, very freaked out, furious
Patrick: Angry

Event 3. The teacher comes over. He wants Patrick to show what's in his pouch.

Omri: Upset, freaked out, frustrated
Patrick: Angry, he didn't get his way, gonna show the teacher

Event 4. Patrick realizes Omri doesn't want Patrick to show the teacher.

Omri: Unhappy, freaked out, nervous
Patrick: Unhappy, worried, scared, sorry

Event 5. Patrick shows the teacher the two "toys."

Omri: Relieved, okay, still a bit nervous
Patrick: Relieved, guilty that he caused the problem

Event 6. Their friendship is okay again and they go off to class.

Omri: Feels okay
Patrick: Feels okay

Figure 8.2. Tracking changes in feeling states during a short scene with Moving Up Mindreaders

Exploring Relationships Between Characters

Detective Head tasks consistently focus on how actions (such as those of a character) influence the thoughts, feelings, and actions of others and how their thinking and acting in response influences the feelings and actions of other characters. Relationships change not only within one scene but usually throughout the course of a movie. Movies are selected for Moving Up Mindreaders because of the nature of the relationships that develop between main characters. The relationships don't always "feel good" — there are conflicts and resolutions. These movies provide an opportunity to discuss how most relationships have these fluxes and that we don't usually abandon a relationship as soon as one thing goes wrong (although some of our students may do just that). For example, students can use a visual tracker to show how the relationship of the two main characters evolves during the course of the movie *Like Mike*. In one of my groups, students combined narrative explanations with drawings of smiling and frowning faces to illustrate the course of the friendship and how it doesn't take off until late in the movie, when Tracy and Calvin feel similar positive feelings toward each other at the same time.

In Detective Head tasks, Moving Up Mindreaders begin to tackle issues of indirectness and politeness, discussed in more detail in "Tackling Indirectness and Other Nuances" later in this chapter. With some tasks, they find they need to go beyond what's said to what's meant. For example, in one scene from *The Indian in the Cupboard*, Little Bear is looking at his house. When Omri compliments him on the finished house, saying it looks fantastic, Little Bear responds with a small smile, "It will do. It is agreeable." With Moving Up Mindreaders, you can follow up with a social question: "Why does Little Bear only say his house is *okay*? Why doesn't he agree with Omri that it looks terrific?" This provides a fitting example of the subtlety and indirectness of language. Little Bear discounts Omri's exclamation because to agree with him would be bragging. His response tells us about Little Bear — he's modest and takes only indirect pride in his work. Because they take the words literally, Moving Up Mindreaders are stumped regularly by scenes like this. When asked what Little Bear means, many of them answer that he "doesn't like his house," "doesn't think he did a good job," or "thinks it's just okay." They fail to understand the meaning behind the message. Detective Head tasks introduce this complicated aspect of social understanding.

Varsity Mindreaders: Making Sense of Relationships

Scenes selected for Varsity Mindreaders are more complex and require much more effort to decode socially. Like Moving Up Mindreaders, Varsity Mindreaders spend a lot of time working on Detective Head tasks when they're required to:

- Consider multiple perspectives concurrently
- Follow opinions and plans of multiple characters
- Explore what's left unsaid
- Break down rapid shifts in feelings
- Follow development of and fluxes in relationships

Varsity Mindreaders generally need less work on language than other Mindreaders. At this level, you'll attend to organization of narrative and probe for complete, precise explanations rather than the structure of their language. You'll want to confirm that students understand the social interactions they're talking about by having them clarify vague answers. To elicit the most detailed descriptions of their social understanding from students, continue to include visual supports in your work, such as lists of feelings and writing down information on a dry-erase board as it's discussed.

Varsity Mindreaders spend much of their time on Detective Head tasks focusing on the interplay between characters and tracking the intent of multiple characters. To do this, they need to remember what they've already learned about the characters as well as the events that occurred in earlier scenes. Students may find it difficult to retrieve information that isn't in the scene they're currently watching, but it's essential for them to understand that each scene builds upon the previous ones. They'll see that events don't occur randomly, and characters' actions don't occur in a vacuum.

Characters in movies used with Varsity Mindreaders usually aren't just "good" or "bad" but are more realistic individuals whose actions can be expected or unexpected and who can make smart as well as poor decisions. As students discuss what happens between characters, they'll explore changes in the relationships, both when they strengthen as well as unravel. Movies for Varsity Mindreaders provide multiple examples of social errors to fuel discussions of "not-so-good" choices that characters make as well as generate ideas of what could have been done differently. Even without making social errors, friendships naturally ebb and flow — issues invariably come up and are resolved one way or another.

Along with the unfolding of relationships over the length of the film, movies at the Varsity Mindreader level contain frequent changes in feeling state. With Detective Head tasks, you ask students to identify significantly more sophisticated emotions, emphasizing the continuum along which emotions move. At this level, students may be intrigued by the fine distinctions between emotion labels, for instance "dreading" versus "panicked," "mischievous" versus "amused," or "explosive" versus "exasperated."

Students may have a vague idea about the definitions of emotion labels but want to know exactly what a word means and enjoy discussing the differences between words. It's helpful to have lists of feelings available for students to use as a reference. You can also identify these words — and give students a break from the movies at the same time — by playing Hangman with emotion vocabulary terms. Somehow it seems that the feeling vocabulary identified through the visual game of Hangman sticks in students' social minds in a productive way.

Figure 8.3 shows a partial list of feelings identified by a group of Varsity Mindreaders as they watched a three-and-a-half minute scene from *Harry Potter and the Order of the Phoenix*. Without visual mediation the activity probably wouldn't have been as complete, the engagement and social interactions as appropriate or rich, or the amount of time the students stayed with the discussion of feelings as long (45 minutes)!

Scene: The Hearing (Harry Potter and the Order of the Phoenix)	
Harry Potter:	Anxious, nervous, relieved, frustrated, hopeful
Cornelius Fudge:	Cocky, confident, arrogant, shocked, worried, incredulous
Dumbledore:	Confident, angry, impatient, assertive, remote

Figure 8.3 Partial list of feelings generated by a group of Varsity Mindreaders

Once a scene is segmented into its components (e.g., Harry entering, reading of the charges, first witness, etc.), students can look at each chunk as a discrete unit in which characters have discrete feelings. For example, Cornelius Fudge doesn't come to a sudden realization that the hearing isn't going as he'd hoped; rather, there's a slow progression to his thoughts that's both informative and interesting. Harry, a relatively passive character in this scene, also has many shifts of emotion. Only after we had completed each part did we look at the gestalt of the scene to discuss the overall experience for each character. Even though the scene is quite short, it's amazing how many feelings it contains!

Tackling Indirectness and Other Nuances

When we examine how we interact, it becomes clear that our words are only part of the communication package. Our true message is often contained not in the words we choose, but in *how* we say them (or even in the words we choose *not* to say). This can include indirectness and subtle nuances that reflect irony, humor, metaphor, innuendo, or sarcasm. Children with social learning limitations constantly struggle to understand indirectness and are confused when criticized for not responding to indirectness correctly. They're also baffled when they're expected to use indirect language themselves.

Varsity Mindreaders working on Detective Head tasks are asked to figure out hidden messages, raising the question: How can we teach indirectness and sophisticated language, such as innuendo and sarcasm, using Movie Time Social Learning? The easiest way is to choose an example and then ask: "She's *saying* x, but she means something else. What do you think she really means?" You may need to take the following actions:

- Help the students recognize when a message has a hidden meaning. Sometimes that means pointing it out.

- Encourage the children to observe the context carefully. Visual information from the scene can tell a lot about what leads up to an indirect statement.
- Support the students in examining facial expressions and nonverbal information. Explain to them that the body frequently tells the true meaning.
- Remind the students to keep in mind what we know about a character because a character's predisposition to act in a certain way can help determine what he or she is trying to say.
- Encourage the children to listen carefully to tone, "how it's said."
- When you're not using Movie Time Social Learning, point out naturally occurring nuanced or indirect language, translating the true meaning (e.g., "Do you have any scissors?" means "I want you to give me scissors.").

As you work on these issues of indirectness and subtlety, you'll come across instances when more than one answer seems to fit, such as whether a character's feelings are somewhere on the sad or on the angry continuum. When such situations arise, you can list the possible emotion labels and encourage students to come up with thoughts for each of the feelings. Then, through your discussions, help the students to recognize that:

- Feelings don't come in isolation.
- We typically have more than one feeling.
- Our thoughts can influence our feelings.
- It can be very difficult to read the minds of others — we just have to use our social smarts to keep making smart guesses.

For all Mindreaders, Detective Head tasks emphasize relationships and feelings through the veil of perspective taking. It's this understanding of the interplay between characters, and the broad range of thoughts and feelings portrayed, that lead quite naturally into discussions about our own similar thoughts, experiences, and feelings. It's those feelings that contribute to empathy, the focus of the next group of tasks, Me Too!

Empathy …
making sure that you can see the world
through somebody else's eyes, stand in their shoes …
that's the basis for kindness and compassion.

– Barack Obama

Chapter 9

PRACTICING Empathy

Me Too! Tasks

Me Too! activities represent the most sophisticated tasks in Movie Time Social Learning, targeting the foundational relationship skills of synchrony and empathy. While many Me Too! tasks focus on empathic understanding for Moving Up and Varsity Mindreaders, these tasks also can plant the seeds of empathy in Junior Mindreaders.

Empathy, of course, is the ability to understand what another person is experiencing and then feeling. We use our perspective taking skills and array of personal experiences in conjunction with our neurological wiring to recognize and relate to the experiences of others. Empathy plays a role in all social relationships. As we interact with each other, we generally want to show empathy or feel empathy from others. However, even the socially adept can make social thinking misjudgments. We've all had experiences in which we've failed to be empathic, when we're told: "You just weren't listening!" "You don't understand me!," "Don't you care?," or "Can't you say something nice?"

Being empathic isn't always easy. While it connects us with another person in ways that expand us as well as the relationship, it also exposes us to uncomfortable feelings, such as when we express empathy in situations when we might also feel envious or when we feel uncomfortable or conflicted.

When we watch movies, most of us have frequent empathic reactions — we cringe during frightening or disgusting scenes and smile during light or pleasant ones. Without any conscious effort on our part, we feel the feelings of the characters as they experience them. When children with social cognitive deficits watch movies, their faces often appear generally immobile and devoid of emotional reaction (although they may react to humor, especially physical comedy). When we ask for personal connection, we may get a more detached, objective commentary rather than the affective mirroring that we may expect. Keep in mind that, overall, individuals with social cognitive challenges process and feel feelings differently than those who are neurotypical, and we have to respect that difference. Just because we don't "see" or "hear" the reaction we expect doesn't mean that the feeling isn't there.

By using Me Too! tasks, you encourage the expansion of empathic awareness and experience, asking students to unearth connections between movie characters and themselves as they:

- Analyze character feelings in detail
- Discuss similar feelings and experiences of their own
- React with empathy in discussions with adults or other students
- Focus on mirroring experiences and expressing empathy

The tasks can be a starting point for sharing personal experiences. Especially with Me Too! tasks, there are pros and cons to working either individually or in groups. Individual work is great with all kids — it allows you to move at a pace that's appropriate to that child as well as to carefully support them as they work with tasks that focus on feelings and personal experience. Individual work is really a group of two — you're there as a partner in the relationship. Working in groups allows students to get support from peers, watch social learning happening around them, and have the opportunity to hear others share information that may be helpful to their emotional and social cognitive growth.

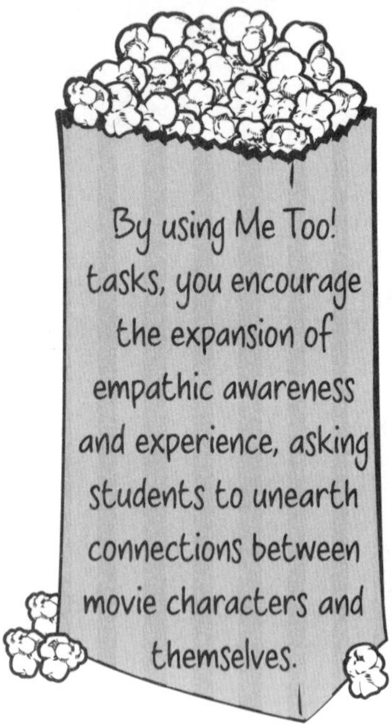

By using Me Too! tasks, you encourage the expansion of empathic awareness and experience, asking students to unearth connections between movie characters and themselves.

Me Too! activities emphasize personal involvement and give students repeated opportunities to experience feelings that arise from an outside source — and from each other — as they begin to relate to people in new, more intimate ways. As you introduce Me Too! tasks to Mindreaders of all levels, you'll find it helpful to take these actions:

- Talk *a lot* about feelings.
- Point out emotional reactions in children as you see them (e.g., "Wow, when you were watching the movie I saw your face look sad/upset/afraid/etc. How were you feeling when you saw that?").

- Give examples from your own life to help students understand what it means to have a similar experience. Whether it's a group or an individual session, modeling the type of narrative you're looking for helps students understand that: (1) this is a safe place to share personal information and (2) it can be hard to talk about situations in which we may have felt uncomfortable. (Sometimes I take some creative license but usually use an actual situation I've experienced.) For example, it took me a while to be able to tell students that I've never jumped into a pool. I explain that it's an embarrassing thing to admit (and to write in a book). Often, such sharing will elicit equally telling stories.
- Encourage students to remember details of their own past experiences (using visual aids to help make comparisons to the characters you're watching).

The following are examples of suggested discussion questions to use during Me Too! tasks. They pertain to the same scenes in the movies presented at the beginning of the previous two chapters for Spy Eye and Detective Head tasks. A full lesson plan for each of these movies is included on the CD. You can use these questions as a model as you prepare to show scenes from other movies to students.

Scene from *No Roses for Harry*

Me Too! Questions for Junior Mindreaders

- If you were Harry, would you tell where the sweater is? Why or why not?
- Have you ever kept a secret like that?
- How do you figure out what to buy someone for a present?

Scene from *The Indian in the Cupboard*

Me Too! Questions for Moving Up Mindreaders

- How would you feel if Omri's experience happened to you? What would you do?
- If you were Omri, would you have shown the dad?
- If you could say something to Little Bear as a friend when he's scared, what would you say?

Scene from *Harry Potter and the Order of the Phoenix*

Me Too! Questions for Varsity Mindreaders

- Have you ever had a teacher who you thought didn't like you or treated you unfairly?
- Have you ever been harassed by kids like Dudley?
- If you were Malfoy's friend, what could you say to him?

Junior Mindreaders: Do You Feel What I Feel?

Junior Mindreaders, with their emerging perspective taking skills, struggle to understand the thoughts and feelings of others. Without that understanding, they have nothing to relate *to.* I like to think of their mirror neurons as needing some glass cleaner. Many of these children can label feelings in themselves but find it difficult to recognize what they look like in others and process what they feel like in others. Feelings are such a complicated affair and can be so illogical at times. For children who think in concrete ways, for whom 1+1=2 is the foundation of how they relate, the murky, uneven, makes-no-sense world of emotions can be so confusing they retreat from even wanting to explore it. So, start by making it an enjoyable experience, showing movies that will help them learn to empathize with feelings that feel good. Whether you're working individually or in a group, celebrate those times when they realize they can figure out how a character feels. For them, empathy begins in that moment when they recognize they share a feeling with a character or another person based on a similar experience. Let that be something good to remember.

Me Too! tasks target the "Yeah, I have that feeling, too!" awareness, looking at both pleasant and, eventually, uncomfortable feelings, some of which are outlined in Figure 9.1 below. Junior Mindreaders who may be just starting to talk about feelings will work on the more basic emotions of sad, angry, and happy (as well as okay). Over time and as their confidence builds, you may be able to introduce the additional feelings of afraid and excited, preparing them to move toward Moving Up Mindreader status. Even though you may not expect students to label the more sophisticated feelings, it's always good to start teaching and differentiating them: "Yes, I think she feels sad — she's sad that she doesn't have Knuffle Bunny. We could use another feeling word for that — disappointed." Me Too! activities ask Junior Mindreaders to think about feelings and experiences common to young children:

- Sadness over loss of something
- Disappointment when certain expectations aren't met
- Frustration at being unable to solve a problem
- Happiness about something good happening
- Fear about a frightening event

Form of empathy	For feelings such as	When someone	Empathic response might be
Expressing concern over the distress (physical or emotional) of others	• Sadness • Disappointment • Anger • Fear	• Falls down • Loses something special • Doesn't get something • Does something that's hard	• "Are you okay?" • "I'll help you find it." • "It's okay." • "You can do it."

Form of empathy	For feelings such as	When someone	Empathic response might be
Shared emotional appreciation of joyful events	• Excitement • Happiness • Pride	• Anticipates something fun • Gets a present he or she loves • Does a great job	• "Wow!" • "Cool!" • "Nice job!"

Figure 9.1. Examples of empathy for Junior Mindreaders

Through doing the Spy Eye and Detective Head tasks, Junior Mindreaders usually have acquired a pretty good sense of what's happened in a scene. They've described events, identified characters' thoughts and feelings, and given opinions about what's happening on screen.

As you work to help students elicit connections between themselves and the characters, it can be helpful to:

- Ask parents or other team member to give you "inside information" (which could be done via a quick email or lunchroom chat)
- Take time to establish details (specific context, characters, issue resolution) when a student offers an example
- Emphasize feeling states
- Use visual aids as needed to "map" the event
- Encourage other students to add their thoughts to another's response (this may turn into an empathic statement)
- Restate similarities between the children's and the character's experiences

The following example shows a Junior Mindreader making such a connection. This child easily came up with a personal experience similar to Trixie's loss of a stuffed animal in *Knuffle Bunny*, connected feeling states, and differentiated how her experience is unique (hers was found, but not in the washer).

Anna: I wonder if you've ever lost anything like Trixie did?

Child: I lost my blankie and I was sad. (*points to sad face*)

Anna: What happened?

Child: I cried and my mommy said, "Oh, honey, it's okay." Then she find it. But it wasn't in the washer.

A supporting visual aid that was used with a group is shown in Figure 9.2, in which three boys answered the question "How would you feel if *your* toy broke?" (This is similar to what happened in the event in the movie.) Each chose a face to use and then all expressed and contrasted how they felt. All listened carefully to each other and agreed that it's possible and okay to feel different ways in the same situation.

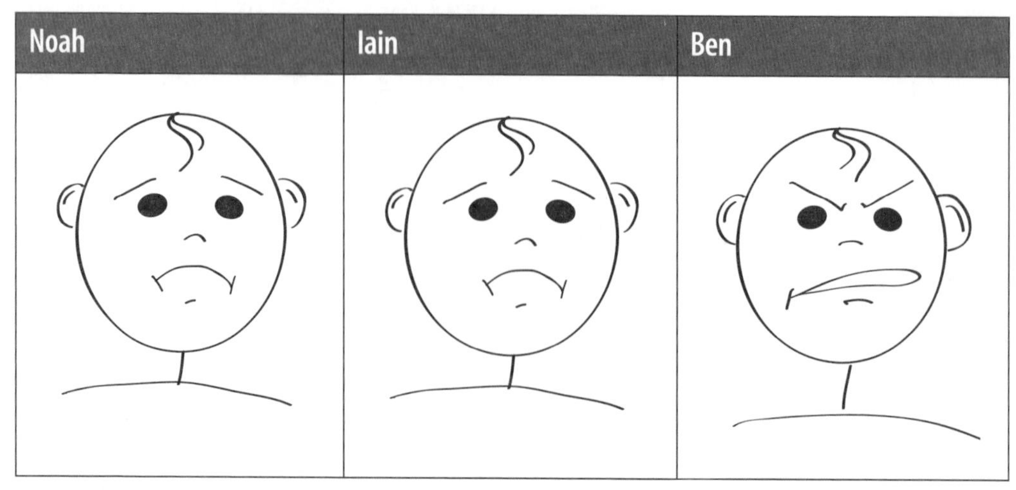

Figure 9.2. Foundational Me Too! activity comparing feelings among Junior Mindreaders

Me Too! tasks, which can be used before or after exploring personal experiences and feelings as a group, often ask the children to generate something they could say to the character. In these instances, the hope is to elicit an empathic statement — one that demonstrates the children understand how the character is feeling and wants to communicate that in a friendly, supportive way. The possibilities in such tasks are infinite.

Children enjoy getting involved in the movie they're watching. If they have trouble, however, you can use visual supports to help them recall the character's feelings and experiences and keep track of their suggestions. For those who are still in the early stages of perspective taking, reflect the situation back: "How would *you* feel in this situation?" Then you can ask, "How would that make the character feel?" Rather than labeling their comments as right or wrong, which can dead end a student's interest and motivation, this sequence helps them expand their awareness of self and others. In any case, you want the children to make that projection themselves, and offer a repair to the original comment if they realize an error. Figure 9.3 offers empathic responses generated by Junior Mindreaders. Notice that some are more empathic than others, but all are connected to the character and situation in a logical way.

Movie	Scene	The character feels	Student responses
Whistle for Willie	The boy can't whistle.	Sad	• "It's okay." • "Keep trying." • "Don't be sad."
Knuffle Bunny	Dad can't find Knuffle Bunny.	Sad and frustrated	• "He can't see it." • "You will find it!" • "Look more."
No Roses for Harry	The bird unravels Harry's sweater.	Happy	• "Yeah!" • "He didn't like it."
Pooh's Grand Adventure: The Search for Christopher Robin	Rabbit sees a scary shadow.	Afraid	• "Don't worry." • "He should run." • "Close his eyes." • "It's okay — I think it's Christopher Robin."

Figure 9.3. Junior Mindreaders responding to the prompt "What could you say to him?"

Aside from what happens in the movies, sessions with children are filled with opportunities to practice empathy. A child may say something terrible happened to him on the playground or another might be excited about her upcoming birthday. You may even have something to share with the group that could use some empathy. Compliment Junior Mindreaders on their great work being empathic, whether it's with a movie character or with each other. Be specific about what they did that was so terrific.

Moving Up and Varsity Mindreaders: "Dude, You Can't Just Say That!"

The principles behind Me Too! tasks at the Moving Up and Varsity levels are the same, so they're discussed here together. Both types of Mindreaders are challenged to think and talk about feelings more deeply than is usual. They're asked to discuss experiences that generate not just pleasant feelings but uncomfortable ones, too. Whether working in groups or with you individually, they're encouraged to listen to others describing what may be difficult events and relate to them based on their own personal experiences, which may be unpleasant as well.

In my work with Moving Up and Varsity Mindreaders on Me Too! activities, I've heard children share many experiences that they've never talked about before. These can serve as jumping-off points for some amazing discussions. You'll need to balance these non-movie based discussions with the actual Movie Time work. While you want to use real life based discussions as the terrific social thinking material that they are, you don't want to get so far afield that everyone forgets what's happening in the movie! Always keep discussions on the social cognitive track (e.g., "That sounds like a very funny story, but can I ask you to talk about how you may have been feeling?").

While most of these students have watched plenty of movies, they usually have very little practice identifying personal connections to characters or their experiences. Discussing emotions may still be a relatively new skill. The work with Detective Head tasks requires that students think and talk about feelings while considering multiple perspectives. Me Too! activities provide a structure in which Moving Up and Varsity Mindreaders practice generating empathic comments for characters, as well as making empathic comments in the moment as spontaneous opportunities arise.

Encourage students to listen carefully to each other. Especially when things get exciting and everyone seems to have something to share, it may be useful to establish a structure for turn taking (perhaps by passing a "talking stick" to the speaker). Cue students to listen not just to the words but to the feelings behind the words as well. Always bring it back to feelings. If an empathic comment works, help the child recognize that it did so because the feeling was properly identified and the delivery suggested caring and concern. If the comment doesn't work or doesn't address the feeling, back up and try to help the student identify or clarify what the character is feeling and/or discuss why the comment might not have been a best guess. And, don't overlook that a great empathic response may be totally nonverbal and a more accurate feeling identification. Once, a boy who I was working with was watching a very moving scene and his face practically melted with empathy. It was clear that he was totally relating at the emotional level. He so appreciated when I pointed out that I could tell how he was feeling and that he looked so empathic with the character. Remember how much empathy we communicate through our facial expressions.

Many Me Too! tasks involve group discussion, which can snowball out of control. Help group members appreciate the quickly changing dynamics by actively using aids, such as nonverbal and verbal prompts (to guide deeper thought), visual records (to track who says what), and restating (to clarify what has been said).

Facilitate ongoing group discussions about shared experiences and feelings — you aren't getting sidetracked from your social thinking work when you do this. You're teaching empathy in the moment of real experiences. Restate at the end how the empathic comments were socially important.

Length of Conversations

You'll find that the length of discussions varies greatly. There may be times when a quick empathic "pop-in" is appropriate. For example, while watching a scene from *Shrek*, I followed up with a question after Tristan identified that Shrek was feeling proud:

Anna: Can you think of a time when you felt proud like Shrek?

Tristan: I was able to build my Legos. I built a robowalker.

Anna: Can you remember how you felt about that?

Tristan: I was happy. I just liked it. I put it down. It's all about work — when you're finished you can be proud. Then you gotta just move on — go on to the next job.

At other times, you'll engage in a longer conversation. There's no rule of thumb about the length of any particular discussion. Some examples are just "meatier" than others, the group may be more or less ready to be empathic at any particular time, or you may or may not want to branch away from the movie — perhaps the other Movie Time Social Learning tasks are moving along smoothly, and you don't want to lose your rhythm. As one of my Varsity Mindreaders would say, "It's all good."

What to Say to a Character

As with all Movie Time Social Learning tasks, you'll find that some students are further along in their social learning than others. This may be particularly evident in tasks when you ask children to generate empathic comments they could make to the characters "if you were there" or "if you were his friend," as illustrated in the following table.

Movie	Scene	Character feeling	Student responses
The Indian in the Cupboard	Little Bear just got shot.	• Sad • Sorry	• "It's okay, you didn't mean it." • "You could have killed him!" • "So what, he's not dead."
The Pink Panther	Clouseau has been arrested and fired.	• Betrayed • Puzzled	• "It's not your fault — it was a stupid mistake." • "That guy's a jerk." • "Hang in there."

Figure 9.4. Empathic comments generated by Moving Up Mindreaders

In general, Moving Up Mindreaders are asked to be empathic to appealing characters. We can sometimes challenge Varsity Mindreaders, however, by asking them to be empathic to very *un*likeable characters. I remind students that even "bad guys" have friends. This tougher task pushes them to follow the steps of the empathic process: Identify the feeling of the character (irrespective of what you may yourself be feeling) and relate to that emotion. An example can be found in a scene in *Harry Potter and the Order of the Phoenix*, in which Bellatrix (one of the worst of the bad) is leaving prison to join up with Voldemort. The group members were able to identify her as feeling "triumphant" and "defiant." So far, great! It was trickier to come up with what they might say if they were escaping with her; this required shifting toward being an unpleasant character themselves. But the group got into it and improved with practice, with examples such as the following ones:

- "Yeah! We got out!" (Nice words, but said deadpan — we needed to talk about it and practice our "nasty and triumphant" tone.)
- "We are the evil conquerors!" (Delivered with appropriate evil-doer tone, that's better.)
- "Voldemort, we are ready!" (They were really getting into it now.)
- "Aaaaaaaaaaahhhhhhhhh!" (Announced with arms in the air; all the kids started doing it and I started to feel under attack myself!)

Whether the Me Too! tasks you're working on are this dramatic or more low-key, you'll have an opportunity to continue your discussions as you:

- Give nonverbal feedback yourself and have students rate various comments as well with a "thumbs up" or "thumbs down," either by you providing the feedback yourself, or more optimally, having students participate in using this simple signal.
- Generate group consensus about various comments.
- Talk about how difficult it can be to be empathic (e.g., when confused or uncomfortable).
- Identify the reasons why some comments don't work.
- Repair comments the group feels aren't appropriately empathic.

In the following example (Figure 9.5), students watch a scene in *Harry Potter and the Order of the Phoenix* in which Harry is feeling nervous about going into the hearing that may result in his expulsion from Hogwarts. They respond to the prompt: "If you were Harry Potter's friend, what would you say to him?"

Pop-in empathy	Group comments
You should tell them about the Dementors.	Good suggestion, but it might not help Harry feel better.
Good luck.	Good — makes it sound like you're with him.
I don't think he should even go — he should just get out of there and go to Hogwarts anyway — it wasn't a big deal.	Don't argue — you're supposed to make Harry feel better.

Figure 9.5. Varsity Mindreaders discussing empathic comments (*Harry Potter and the Order of the Phoenix*)

Building Empathy

Me Too! tasks can take time. When a teachable moment arises spontaneously, taking advantage of it can provide important generalization work. In the example that follows, I worked with two middle-school boys who, although they had been in a group together for a while, hadn't developed much of a relationship. They both had demonstrated relatively high conversational skills, but in social situations they were only marginally empathic. The discussion about *Harry Potter and the Order of the Phoenix* went on for about five minutes, during which I took advantage of the fact that I'd been on crutches for several months to find an entry point into some wonderfully appropriate empathy. I used several mediating strategies in this discussion: open-ended questions, the dry-erase board, restating, and cuing attention to details.

In the movie scene we'd just watched, Hermione helps Ron, who is in danger. Both boys watched this scene with relatively deadpan expressions. As we started our discussion, the mail happened to come through my mail slot in my office. Anthony got up and brought me the mail with a smile while Orin watched.

Anna: Thanks! That was so kind of you to get the mail. You just helped me, kind of like Hermione helped Ron. Can you talk about what you were thinking when you did that? (*Orin has not shown through facial expression or language that he had any particular thought about what Anthony did. I wanted to use this to connect with what we had just seen onscreen.*)

Anthony led as all three of us generated a list on the dry-erase board:

- It must be bad to be on crutches.
- I felt sad for you.
- I wanted to help you out because you have crutches.
- I felt sorry for you.
- I figured you could use help because it's hard for you to do these things.

Anna: It sounds like you were thinking about what it's like for me to be on crutches. You were being empathic. Can you think of a time that someone helped you?

Anthony: (*Orin listens.*) Yeah — I fell off my bike in the bushes and hurt my knee. (*Orin cringed; I asked Anthony how he felt.*) I felt unhappy, scared, and sad. (*I asked him what he wanted.*) I felt like I wanted to get out of the bushes, for Mom to help me — and she did — she pulled me out. (*Orin smiled and nodded.*)

Anna to Orin: What do you think about Anthony's story? (*His demeanor has shown empathy and I wanted to see if he could expand his response to include language.*)

Orin: Hey, I can relate! That sounds like it hurt! You're lucky your mom was there to help you! (*Anthony nodded, with a rueful smile.*)

Anna to Anthony: Have you ever been in a situation like that but where you helped your mom? (*I wanted to see if he could reverse roles.*)

Anthony: Yeah! Mom was sick and I made her breakfast in bed. (*I asked what he was thinking.*) I felt she would appreciate it and like it. I felt happy 'cuz it was nice to help my mom when she was needing help.

Orin: That was really nice — I bet she liked that! (*Spontaneous empathy — just what this activity is looking for!*)

Anna: (*after a bit more discussion about Ron also feeling like he needed help*) Let's watch the part with Hermione again. Pay attention to how she feels helping him and how Ron felt when she did. (*Both boys watched carefully with more animated faces — concern, then weakly smiling, nodding.*)

Orin: Yeah, it's kind of how Anthony just helped you. (*Anthony grins.*)

Many children inevitably will struggle as you work together on the empathy-in-the-moment tasks. That's one of the characteristics of individuals with social learning challenges. That's one of the reasons you're working with them. However, while it's one thing to hear abrasive, brusque, nonempathic responses generated during movie viewing, it can be quite another to hear these during a live, engaged conversation.

So what do you do when a child offers a socially inappropriate response? Sometimes it may be funny, but at other times they might actually be hurtful. I remember telling a group that my dog had died only to hear a student say "I'm so sorry — was she small enough that you could flush her down the toilet?" When this happens:

- *Don't overreact!*
- Help everyone regain a well-regulated state if you feel that's warranted.
- Go over the social error in a gentle and non-judgmental way — remember, these comments are usually not made out of malice or the desire to "crack everyone up" (although…).
- Remind everyone that we all make mistakes from time to time, and if in a group, ask others to talk about similar social mistakes they may have made. That may generate natural empathy.
- Base your discussion in *feelings* (e.g., "Hmmm, how do you think what you just said makes me feel?").
- Move on!

Next Steps

Now that you've learned about mediating strategies as well as about the different types of tasks involved with Movie Time Social Learning, you're ready to choose your movies and get the popcorn ready.

You can never step into the same river;
for new waters are always flowing on to you.

– Heraclitus of Ephesus

Chapter 10

Off and Running

Generalizing What Students Have Learned

No matter which tools and techniques we use to expand students' social thinking abilities, we ultimately want them to show their new knowledge in naturally occurring situations. We want learners to take freshly acquired ideas and apply these at home, at a friend's house, on family trips, at the mall, concerts, museums — that's to say, *everywhere.* That's our paramount goal.

Of course, there are challenges leading up to this important step. We know that children with social learning difficulties struggle to generalize what they learn in one context to another, such as taking a skill from the therapy room to the playground, classroom, or home (Crooke, Hendrix, & Rachman, 2007).

Laying the Groundwork: Principles of Generalization

Movie Time Social Learning guides students to think and talk about relationships in ways that are key to developing social understanding. The program's tasks allow them to practice making sense of social interactions and forming connections to their own lives.

While it's heartening to see children blossom as social thinkers during Movie Time Social Learning and actively engage in discussion about movie-character interactions, we constantly need to think about ways to help them expand these social thinking abilities into everyday situations.

We've enjoyed watching and talking about movies together. Now we're responsible for guiding generalization so they can take skills demonstrated in one context and apply them to new situations. This involves:

- Understanding similarities between contexts
- Identifying and modifying past responses to similar situations retrieved from our episodic memory (bank of past experiences)
- Applying our best social guess in the moment
- Making continued refinements based on feedback we receive

We want to increase their chances of social success by concentrating on generalization activities as part of our daily work with budding social thinkers. Like much of the work aiming to address social learning challenges, the Movie Time Social Learning program emphasizes:

- Thinking with your eyes about the world
- Considering multiple perspectives
- Expanding feelings vocabulary
- Understanding nonverbal information
- Empathizing with others
- Developing narrative language skills needed to express the complexities of social interactions

These can be communicated in many forms. An informal meeting with a group of parents or a teacher workshop can transmit a lot of information in a relatively short period while promoting face-to-face discussion. Less desirable are letters or reading references distributed without discussion. Though I prefer to transmit information in person, there are times when that avenue just isn't available. In that case, a follow-up email or phone call is important because it's through further discussion that a more comprehensive understanding of Social Thinking theory develops. Then parents and other team members will be able to facilitate activities more fluidly and make thoughtful observations, for example:

- "I realized I was always telling David what I was thinking … When I stopped doing it for him and gave him time to think, he really did figure it out himself."
- "I never thought of feelings on a continuum — it makes so much sense…"
- "We visited my mom in the hospital yesterday. I was shocked when Katie said how hard it must be for Grandma to be away from home — she never, ever said stuff like that before we started talking about connecting with how others feel."

Building Understanding: Using the Mediating Tools

The mediating strategies in Chapters 4 to 6 are effective at encouraging broader social thinking. Review these strategies (e.g., silence, gesture, facial expressions, visual supports, etc.) with others who work with the students. Give examples of how you use them, and share what changes you notice as a result. Acknowledge that implementing these strategies requires practice and that some of our more habitual behaviors (e.g., talking too much, giving the answer rather than helping the child discover it) are, in fact, not very helpful.

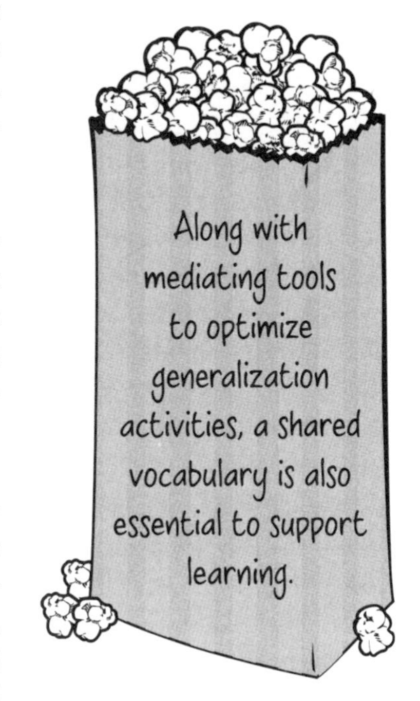

It's instructive to demonstrate how you use these strategies in practice while pointing out how they support the student. There's nothing like a live demonstration to show how much silence may be necessary before a budding social thinker figures things out and can produce a socially thought-out answer.

Along with mediating tools to optimize generalization activities, a shared vocabulary is also essential to support learning. When students hear consistent terminology being used, it eliminates any guesswork (e.g., whether two similar terms mean the same thing) and makes it easier for them to demonstrate their social thinking abilities. Generating a list of Social Thinking vocabulary that everyone understands and uses makes it easier for students to recognize that it really is just one big world out there — that, while every situation is unique, there are global similarities that can guide our social actions. The words can be at least one constant in their ever-changing social world.

Strength in Numbers: Gathering Your Team

The fastest and most complete generalization of Social Thinking will happen using a team approach. Harnessing everyone available to be on the "Social Thinking bandwagon," reinforcing the same vocabulary, and noticing changes in thinking and behavior as well as challenges that still need to be addressed give the message to everyone (including the child) that these skills are valuable *in all situations*.

A team may include:

- Parents
- Teachers, resource staff, and classroom aides
- Occupational and physical therapists
- Speech therapists
- Psychotherapists
- Babysitters
- Siblings and extended family
- Anyone else with whom the student regularly spends time

As the person working most intensively on social thinking abilities, it's your responsibility to coordinate continuing efforts as you:

- Make sure everyone has effective tools to elicit maximum social thought
- Support the team members in changing their own thinking and behaviors
- Suggest activities to structure hands-on practice
- Encourage and answer questions
- Initiate check-in from time to time
- Elicit information about areas/situations that continue to be challenging
- Remember to appreciate everyone's efforts

Generalization is supported when adults notice successes as well as challenges and increase their own awareness of Social Thinking concepts.

Broaden Your View:
Using Familiar Materials in New Ways

Before you can expect students to generalize the work in one situation to another, you need to generalize the work *within* whatever context you're working. You need to inculcate *all* of your interactions with Social Thinking ideas. The more you expand the way you work, the more ideas you'll have to share with other members of the team.

Remember that social situations occur all the time, including in the therapy room, on the playground, and at home. Many wonderful materials available to expand social thinking abilities — the books published by Winner's Social Thinking Publishing as well as interactive software to expand emotional understanding by Baron-Cohen and others — provide excellent tools to expand conversations about social engagement. A number of these publications and materials are listed in Appendix C.

When using Movie Time Social Learning, experiment with some of the following ideas (you're probably doing so already!):

- Many children's books are exceptionally well suited for practice in identifying thoughts, feelings, and plans of characters. Apply the Movie Time activity breakdowns to events in books. You can do this with children in preschool through high school if you dig for the right book. See Appendix C for a list of my favorites.
- This book presents a limited selection of movies. Scout for others to watch and discuss. I encourage middle-school and high school–age students to share movie scenes about relationships that they think are interesting in some way. Note the ratings, however — *never* R-rated.
- Working with sequence cards? Take a minute to include social thinking processes by asking about thoughts, feelings, and plans. Don't forget to elicit empathic comments in response to the pictures. Image of a broken toy or

unhappy situation? Discuss solutions to the problem, but also ask students what they would say if it happened to a friend. Go slower but deeper through your general social language–building activities.

- Playing a game to practice turn taking? Practice flexibility with older elementary, middle school, and high school students by adding a "rule change" component in which everyone takes a turn to develop new rules for the game — use those rules for one minute, then it's another person's turn to change the rules. Have players rotate so they play from someone else's position or with a different set of cards. This never fails to elicit lots of feelings and thoughts! Some games are based in social thinking more than others. For a list of ones I like, refer to Appendix C.
- Need materials from the shelf? Stay seated and try to communicate to a child nonverbally what you'd like him or her to get them. Use drama and humor to keep the guesses coming.
- If you're working on verbal problem-solving, discuss the social repercussions of various solutions. Students find it easier to determine negative consequences than positive ones (e.g., "others will have good thoughts"). Often they say that "nothing" will happen. Not true! Always emphasize that there are *consequences to all action, even inaction.*

Opportunity Knocks: Finding Material in Everyday Life

The best examples to teach social thinking are found in real life. Situations that you either witness yourself or have been described to you by a reliable source can provide a treasure trove of material!

Look for rich, everyday problems to solve with your Social Thinking groups. Always try to take advantage of any opportunity that falls into your lap during a session. Don't feel you're getting sidetracked; by using real examples you're moving the children forward — another step closer to generalization.

Using such examples as they occur is more effective when you slow the session's overall pace. Keep in mind that many students with social thinking deficits process information slowly, and that social thinking about situations in which they're involved themselves is particularly challenging. Nurture a sense of sensitive collaboration so they feel safe talking about their challenges and social missteps. And remember your visual aids!

Even a minor incident can provide excellent material. In a session with two young boys, a cup of marbles we'd used for another activity accidentally spilled all over the floor. The two boys thought it was funny but were giving only short phrase descriptions ("the marbles fall," "get them"). I could have, of course, quickly picked up the marbles and returned to our interrupted work. However, because both boys were focusing on the spill, it made more sense to engage them in active, interpersonal problem-solving. With the use of the Critical Thinking Triangle as visual support, we were able to develop complex language to discuss the situation and solution. The boys were more engaged with each other during this offshoot activity than they'd been in the original task, and they thoroughly enjoyed their shared appreciation of the moment.

Many day-to-day problems are solved quickly by neurotypical adults and children. As parents, we might hurry to find two matching socks or put the melting ice cream back in the freezer. As therapists, we might quickly tape up a page in a book that has just torn, taking a minute out of the session while the children finish up a game. We don't recognize that children with social thinking difficulties often are oblivious to the processes of critical thinking and problem-solving that occur around them. Because they miss the process, they miss exposure to the complex thought that goes into recognizing and solving the problem.

Give students opportunities to figure out what *you* are thinking and feeling. Show how you feel through facial expression first and ask them to make a smart social guess about what you're thinking. Slow the pace and support them in using their social thinking to formulate a complex sentence to explain how their behavior influenced your thoughts.

Include feelings in (almost) everything and encourage specific feeling labels. When you ask students how they're doing before work begins, remember that "okay" is a feeling. Remind children that when they go out to the waiting room or classroom, other parents, adults, and children will be having thoughts and feelings about them. (It never ceases to amaze me how many students are surprised about this!)

Continue using the mediating strategies you practice with Movie Time Social Learning, and start to develop your own visual aids to support social thinking. Keep your dry-erase board nearby for a quick sketch or sentence. If you use any formal supports to build language (picture strips, Story Grammar Marker, etc.), pull them into your impromptu social discussions. They will be helpful aids for organizing thought.

Think back to the pause and rewind buttons in Movie Time tasks. Though it's impossible to slow the world down and discuss each situation, we can help to promote social thinking by breaking down these socially based, problem-solving strategies in the moment. Use your recording device frequently. Recordings of students playing games, engaging in conversation, or just hanging out can become mini-movies, available for evaluation and discussion just as the commercial movies are.

Making Connections: Communicating with Home and School

Pull what you can from the lives of the children. I always encourage parents to email me descriptions of social events. Similarly, I ask classroom teachers and school staff to describe classroom and playground situations when they arise. I can pull this information to use in my sessions as well as to support parents and staff in facilitating social thinking.

One child I worked with loved to grow his hair out in a wonderful, thick, curly pompadour, which seemed to stand up about a foot on his head. He and his father frequently argued about the need for a haircut. Ryan had trouble understanding his dad's perspective. I spent some time with him exploring how he could think about and determine the opinions held by his family members and me about various issues, ending with his hairstyle. He tried hard to make his best guesses.

In the past, Ryan had worked to identify and accept opinions different from his own in Movie Time Social Learning tasks. This was similar work but applied to members of his family. Our final table (Figure 10.1) supported discussion of the contrasting perspectives about Ryan's hair and helped him understand that a compromise on length might be reasonable. Again, we worked up to the issue at hand and used a visual support to stay on track with our progress. His parents followed up at home, adding columns to the table and continuing to encourage Ryan to figure out "who thinks what."

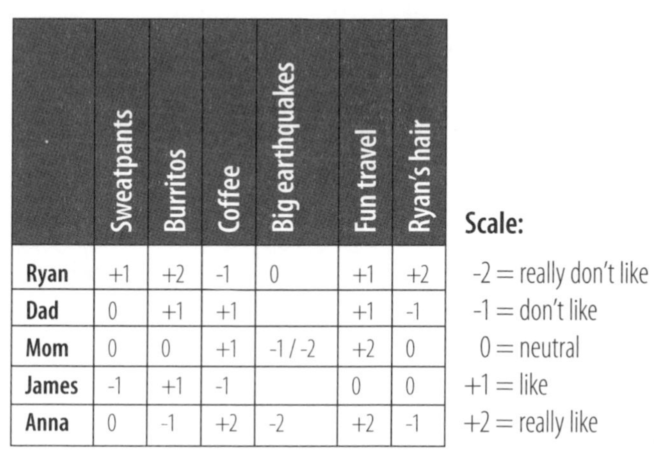

	Sweatpants	Burritos	Coffee	Big earthquakes	Fun travel	Ryan's hair
Ryan	+1	+2	-1	0	+1	+2
Dad	0	+1	+1		+1	-1
Mom	0	0	+1	-1 / -2	+2	0
James	-1	+1	-1		0	0
Anna	0	-1	+2	-2	+2	-1

Scale:
-2 = really don't like
-1 = don't like
0 = neutral
+1 = like
+2 = really like

Figure 10.1. Ryan's scale of opinions (mine and his family's) on different topics

Take your time processing these types of events with children. Use your visual supports to mediate them in figuring out thoughts, feelings, and reactions of others involved.

Another time, I was working with some ninth-grade boys in a Social Thinking group. There had been a school field trip the day before, and I heard that the drive back "didn't go well." These students had, surprisingly, all been in the same car. While that unfortunate coincidence hadn't helped matters, it certainly provided rich therapy material as we reviewed expected and unexpected behaviors to decide how the driver might have felt. Here was their list:

Unexpected behaviors		Expected behaviors
• Biting others	• Complaining to the extreme	• Put on seat belts.
• Choking others	• Cussing	• One person slept.
• Stealing phones	• Punching	• We got out of the car.
• Yanking seat belts	• Tickling	• We didn't damage the car.
• Weirdo noises	• Holding breath contest	
• Prank calls	• Laughing at driver	

Figure 10.2. First field trip behaviors

I kid you not — who could make up a list like this? The driver became so frazzled that she drove over the wrong bridge, adding 45 minutes to the trip. It took our entire session for the guys to develop and *think* about this list, as well as the consequences of their behaviors. They finally determined that, while they enjoyed the fun, the driver must have been feeling "tired," "pissed off," and "upset." Her son confirmed that she hadn't been in a good mood later that evening. They began to understand how she might never want to drive on a field trip again.

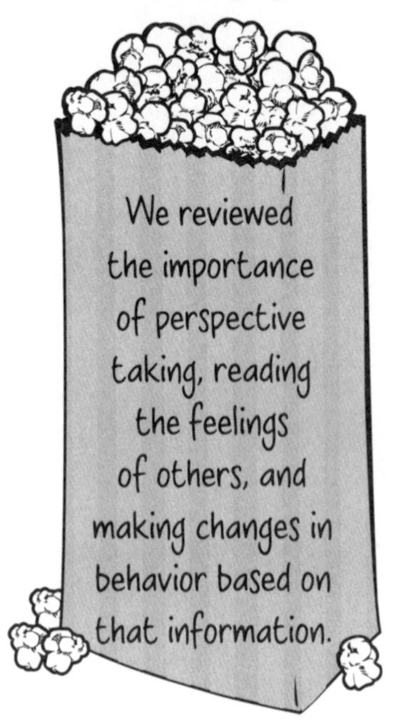

Two weeks later came another field trip. This one consisted of a shorter drive, hike, and pool party. Great — lots of potentially disregulating situations, such as heat, altitude, exertion, and exuberant pool antics. We had a chance to preview the trip and identify possible challenges and their desire to give peers and adults "good thoughts" this time. We reviewed the importance of perspective taking, reading the feelings of others, and making changes in behavior based on that information. Off they went.

The next day I was greeted by an administrator in the hallway with "I *have* to tell you about the trip..." Yikes; I braced myself. She described how wonderful the students had been, especially at the pool party. I kept waiting for the other shoe to drop. It never did. That morning, we inventoried expected and unexpected behavior:

Unexpected behaviors	Expected behaviors
• Well, two teachers raced each other on the drive back to school. • One student admitted that maybe he shouldn't have pushed another group member in the pool so many times.	• Played nicely • Showed off how fast they could eat but it wasn't too gross • Participated in hike all the way • Stopped annoying behavior when asked the first time • Had appropriate fun • Were flexible when some plans changed

Figure 10.3. Second field trip behaviors.

What a difference! Although I suspect there may have been a few more unexpected behaviors than they mentioned, we used this list to review how demonstrating expected behaviors had rewarded the boys as well as those around them. Some of their comments reflected that they'd noticed the positive feedback at the time it was given, both from peers and adults. The boys were extremely pleased with how their behavior had given everyone many good thoughts.

Pulling from Your Own Life: Cultivating Everyday Empathy

In Movie Time Social Learning, all Mindreaders, at various levels of sophistication, are encouraged to express empathy. *As appropriate to the age of the child*, I pull from personal experiences as bait for empathy, announcing beforehand, "I'm going to tell you something about myself and ask you to be empathic about it."

Group or individual work is a wonderful time to work on empathy because students with social thinking difficulties need a supportive environment in which to make their mistakes. These experiences provide material for group discussion and group support because most of the other children present probably have made similar mistakes.

Within reason, I pull examples from my own life, such as feeling sick, dealing with a family problem, planning a personal celebration, or feeling excited about an upcoming event. This shows the children how empathy can be expressed for positive as well as negative situations.

Children with social thinking difficulties tend to not notice the happenings in the lives of those around them. I've worked with high school students who couldn't tell me a single stressor their parents were experiencing and an elementary-age child who couldn't say what a parent might like for a gift. I believe these children benefit from, and in fact require, direct exposure to such situations. I encourage parents to share their personal experiences, plan shopping excursions together, and verbalize how they support each other (e.g., "Sounds like Dad had a hard week — let's make his favorite steak today to help him feel better").

Model, model, model for parents, teachers, and staff who work with your budding social thinkers. It's the best tool for generalization. The more live examples you use and demonstrate, the more they'll understand the principles of your work. When you can, explain the activities you've completed to your team and suggest ways to spread the information into home and classroom.

Using Movie Time Social Learning at Home

As a parent, you may have heard about Movie Time from a teacher or therapist, or even come across it on your own. A great way to start using this program at home is first to review the mediating strategies and think about how you may be able to apply some of the strategies (e.g., more silence) in everyday activities. If your child is receiving language services, talk with the therapist for any input into the appropriate level of Mindreader for your child as well as to get specific information about what might be best to work on, such as reading minds or perspective taking. Get one of the movies and see what happens. Remember, your child may be used to watching movies at home independently, and without stopping every tiny bit, so bring your flexibility along with your clicker! You may want to start in a pretty casual way — just a few minutes at a time, with lots of appreciation of super social thought.

Consider how you can apply Spy Eye, Detective Head, and Me Too! tasks to everyday life. If your child goes to a movie with a family member or friend, try to talk about relationships aspects of the movie (okay, not so easy with those middle and high school students, but give it a quick try). Talk about differing perspectives, whether between characters in a book or movie, kids on the softball team, or family members deciding where they want to go to dinner. Whether you've had a "good" or "bad" day, consider sharing your experiences with your child, giving him or her the opportunity to dig up some empathy. Remember to appreciate your child's empathy, as well as all his or her social thinking efforts. It's not as easy for them as it is for you and me.

Final Thoughts

From my office I can hear a parent in my waiting room saying, "Hmmm, I'm thinking about your shoes," cuing her son to take off his sneakers because they aren't allowed in the therapy room. Another mom reports, "I've been trying to have Sam say what my plans are without telling him. At first he was clueless, but we waited, and like you said, he came up with some pretty good answers." A student starts a conversation with a fellow group member instead of going to read a book in the corner. A teacher emails me with a question about the difference between "whole-body listening" and "listening with your ears." These are signs of children being supported in expanding their social thinking in all aspects of their lives — the true mark of slow and steady generalization.

British philosopher Colin McGinn, in his writings on movies, describes how "the screen functions like a window onto a world beyond." In a similar fashion, Movie Time Social Learning guides children to see their world in new ways, assimilate new concepts into their everyday experiences, and become more competent, skilled social thinkers wherever they are.

Some people are born to sit by a river.
Some get struck by lightning.
Some have an ear for music.
Some are artists. Some swim.
Some know buttons. Some know
Shakespeare.
Some are mothers.
And some people dance.

– The Curious Case of Benjamin Button

Appendix A

Visual Aids

This appendix includes a variety of visual aids you can use with students to support Movie Time Social Learning. Some of these items, such as lists of conjunctions, can be used as is. Others are templates to which you or students add text or drawings. A filled-out example is included for each of the six Tracker Templates.

You can print or photocopy any item in this appendix, put it in a sheet protector, and add card stock or cardboard pieces to make it sturdier. Once in the sheet protector, you can write on the sheet protector with thin-point dry-erase markers during your sessions. The document can then be erased and used again.

When you work with groups or want a large surface, you can add any list or template directly to a dry-erase board with markers.

For more information about using these and other visual tools and to see examples of how these tools have been used with my students, see Chapter 5.

The visual aids included in this appendix are:

- Emotions Strips
  - Basic Four Emotions — Pictorial (for Junior Mindreaders)
  - Expanded Six Emotions — Pictorial (for Junior Mindreaders and Moving Up Mindreaders)

- Basic Four Feelings List (for Junior Mindreaders)
- Expanded Six Feelings List (for Junior and Moving Up Mindreaders)
- Feelings Scale — Circles (for Junior Mindreaders)
- Tracker Templates
    - Idea and Opinion Tracker
    - Empathy Tracker
    - Opinions Tracker
    - Event, Thought, and Feelings Tracker
    - Problem and Options Tracker
    - Event and Feelings Tracker
- Conjunctions Lists

Basic Four Emotions – Pictorial

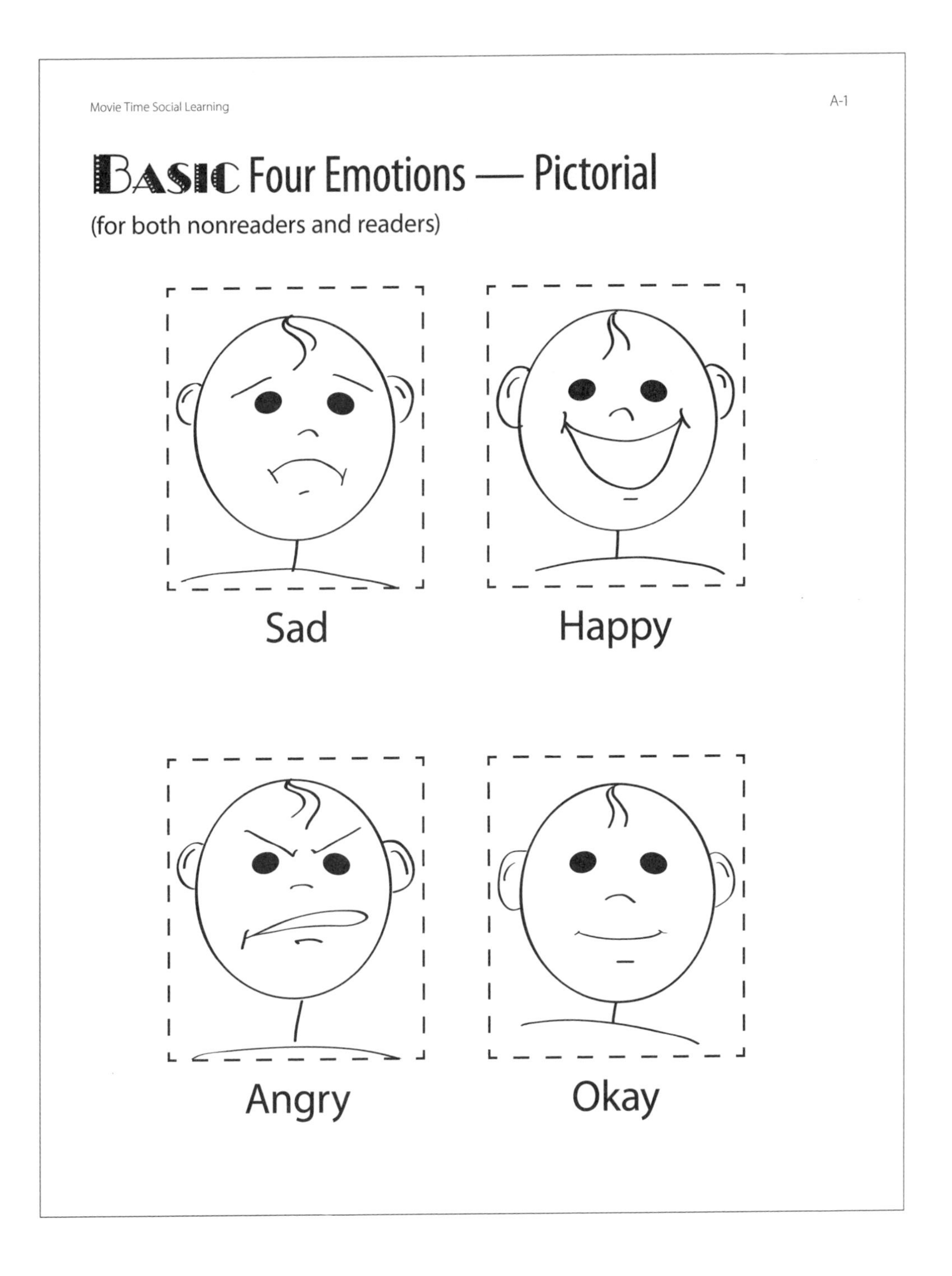

Expanded Six Emotions – Pictorial

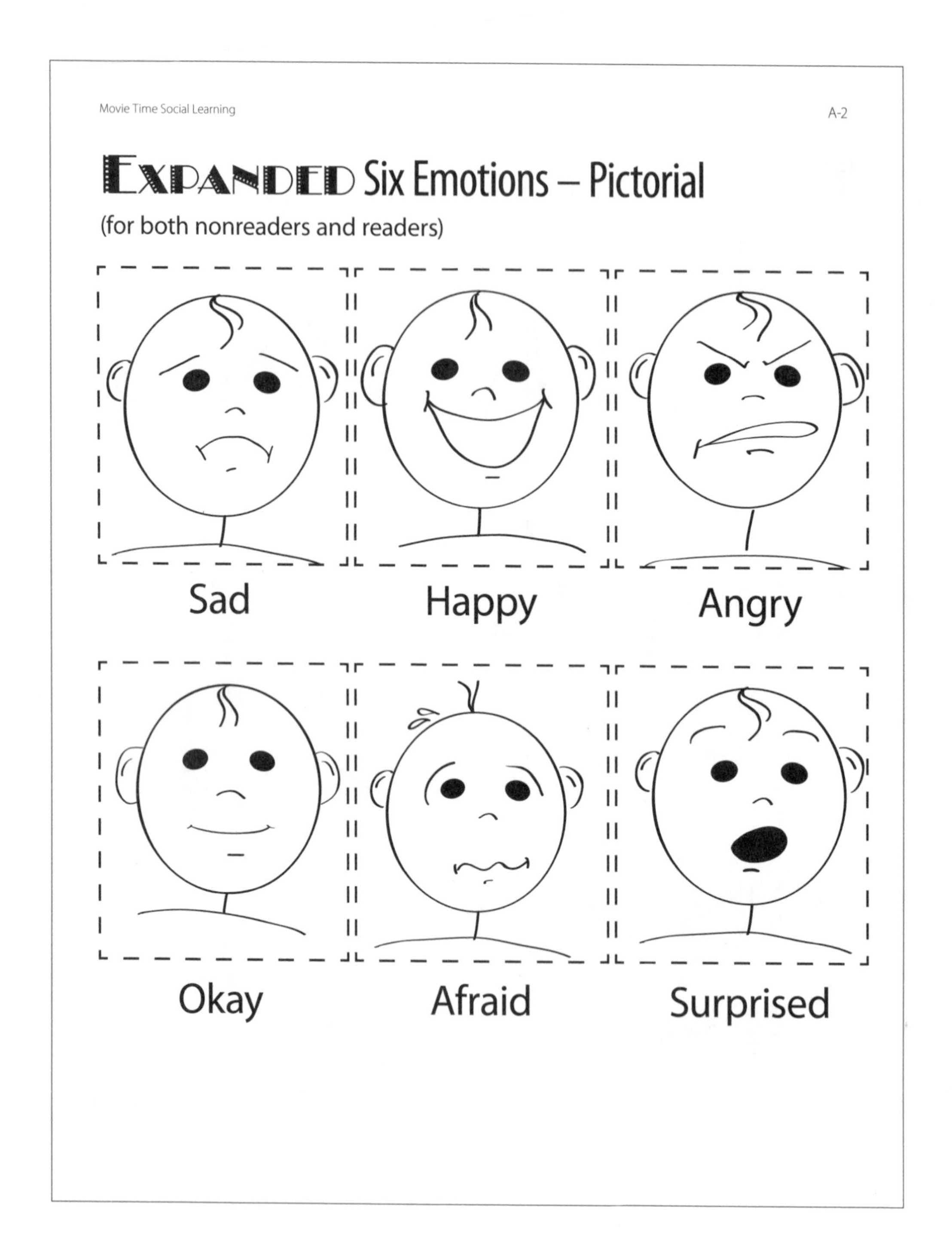

Basic Four Feelings List – Printed Word

Movie Time Social Learning

A-3

BASIC Four Feelings List – Printed Word

(for readers)

sad
happy
angry
okay

Expanded Six Feelings List – Printed Word

Movie Time Social Learning

A-4

EXPANDED Six Feelings List – Printed Word

(for readers)

sad
happy
angry
okay
afraid
surprised

Feelings Scale

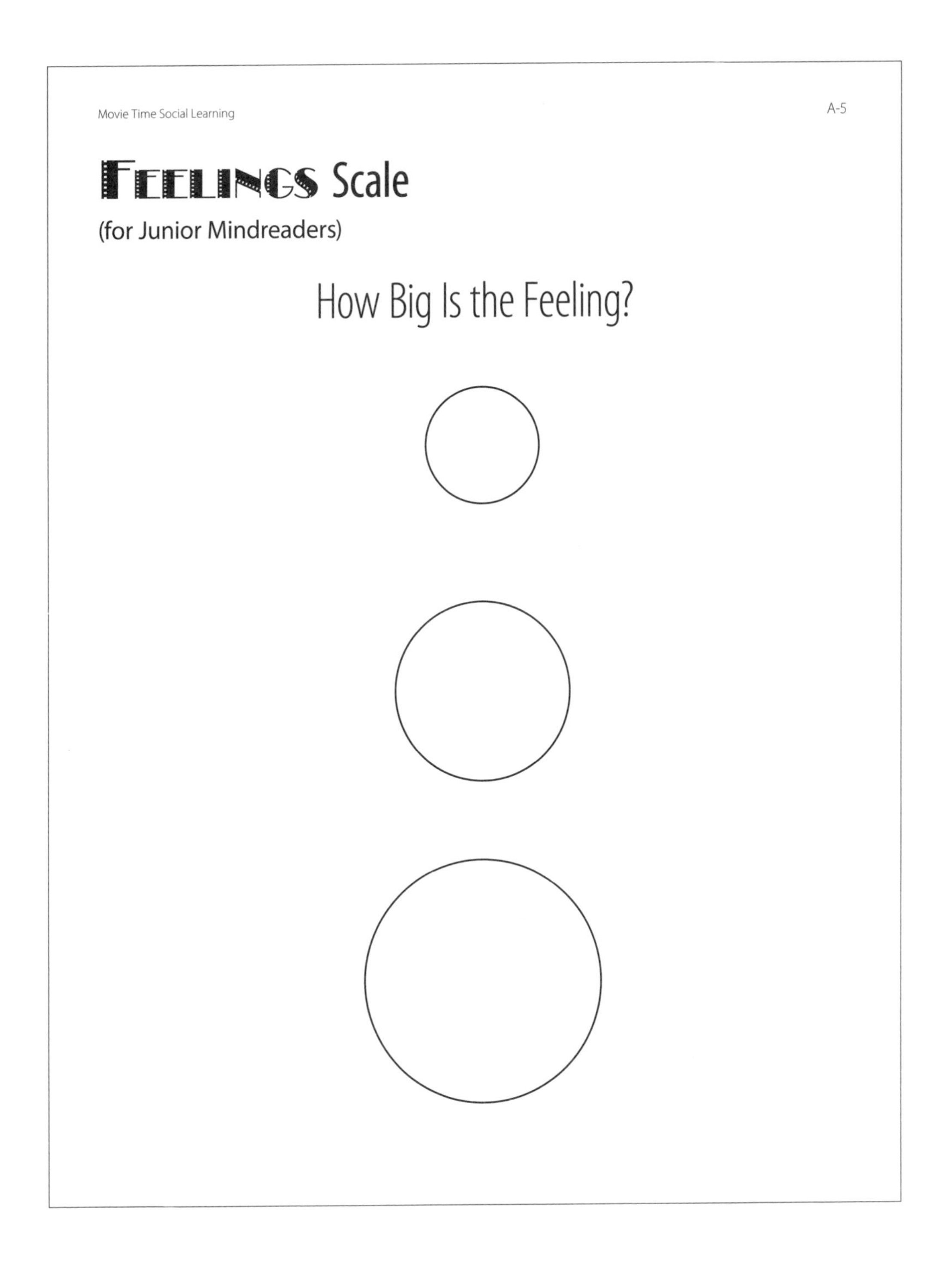

Idea and Opinion Tracker Template

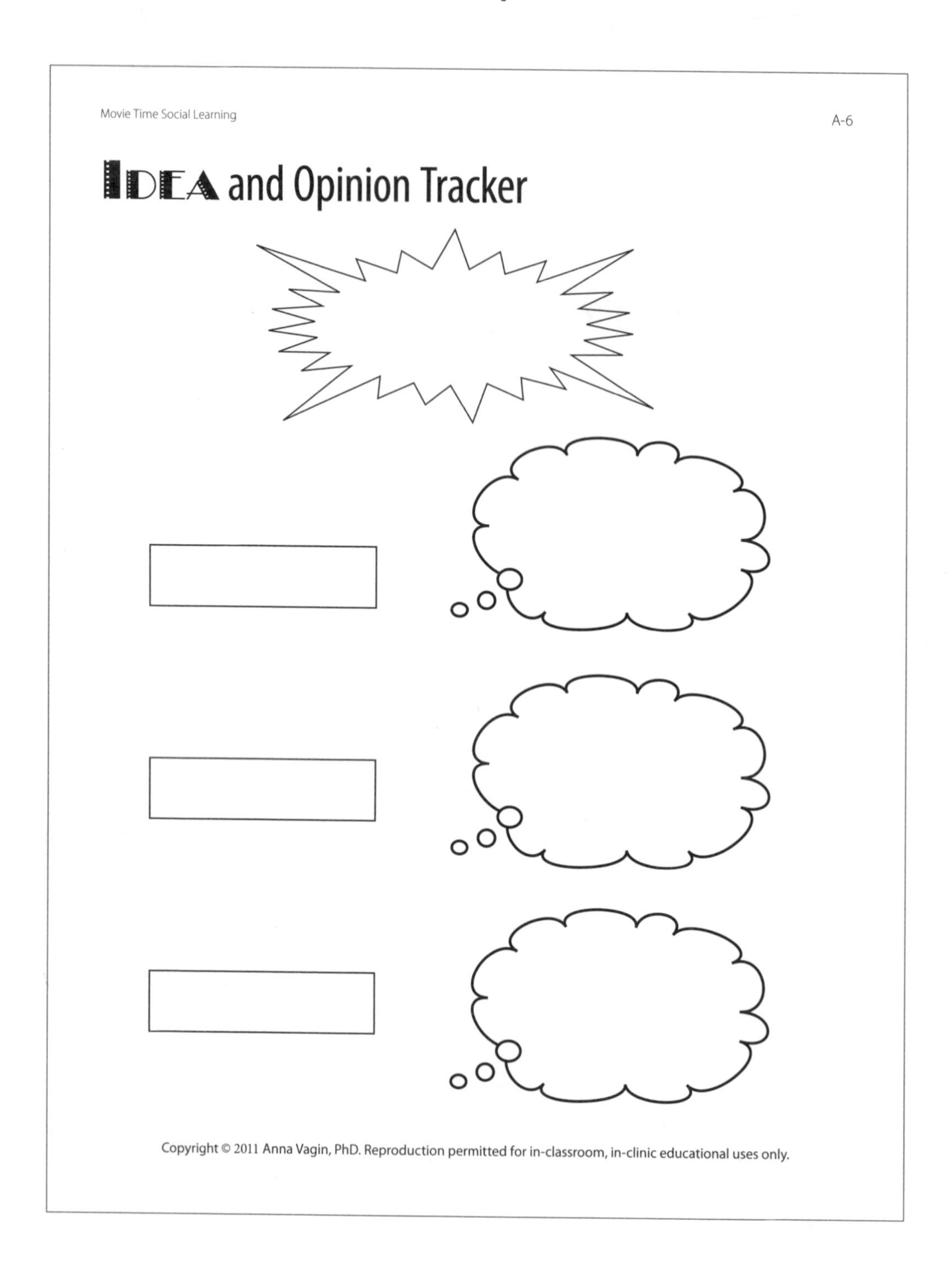

Example of a completed Idea and Opinion Tracker for Junior Mindreaders, from *Whistle for Willie,* Part 1.

Empathy Tracker Template

Example of a completed Empathy Tracker for Junior Mindreaders, from *No Roses for Harry,* Part 1

Opinions Tracker Template

Movie Time Social Learning

A-10

OPINIONS Tracker

Example of a completed Opinions Tracker for Junior Mindreaders, from *Frog Goes to Dinner*, Part 2

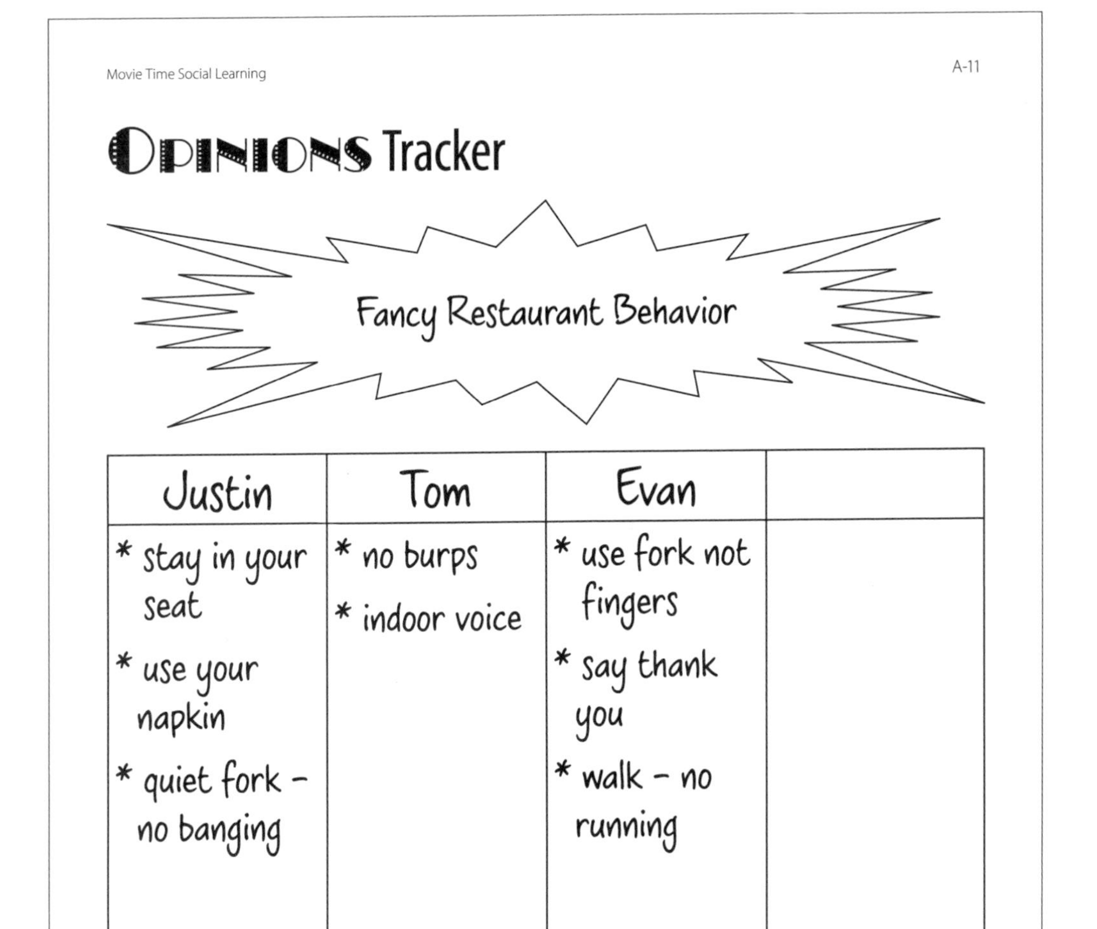

OPINIONS Tracker

Fancy Restaurant Behavior

Justin	Tom	Evan	
* stay in your seat * use your napkin * quiet fork - no banging	* no burps * indoor voice	* use fork not fingers * say thank you * walk - no running	

Event, Thought, and Feelings Tracker Template

Event, Thought, and Feelings Tracker

Character 1

Character 2

Example of a completed Event, Thought, and Feelings Tracker for Varsity Mindreaders, from *Harry Potter and the Order of the Phoenix*, Scene 13.

Problem and Options Tracker Template

PROBLEM and Options Tracker

What to Do?

Character:

Social Problem (include feelings):

Final Rating

Option 1.

Consequences (include feelings):

Option 2.

Consequences (include feelings):

Option 3.

Consequences (include feelings):

Option 4.

Consequences (include feelings):

Example of a completed Problem and Options Tracker for Junior Mindreaders, from *Frog Goes to Dinner*, Part 3.

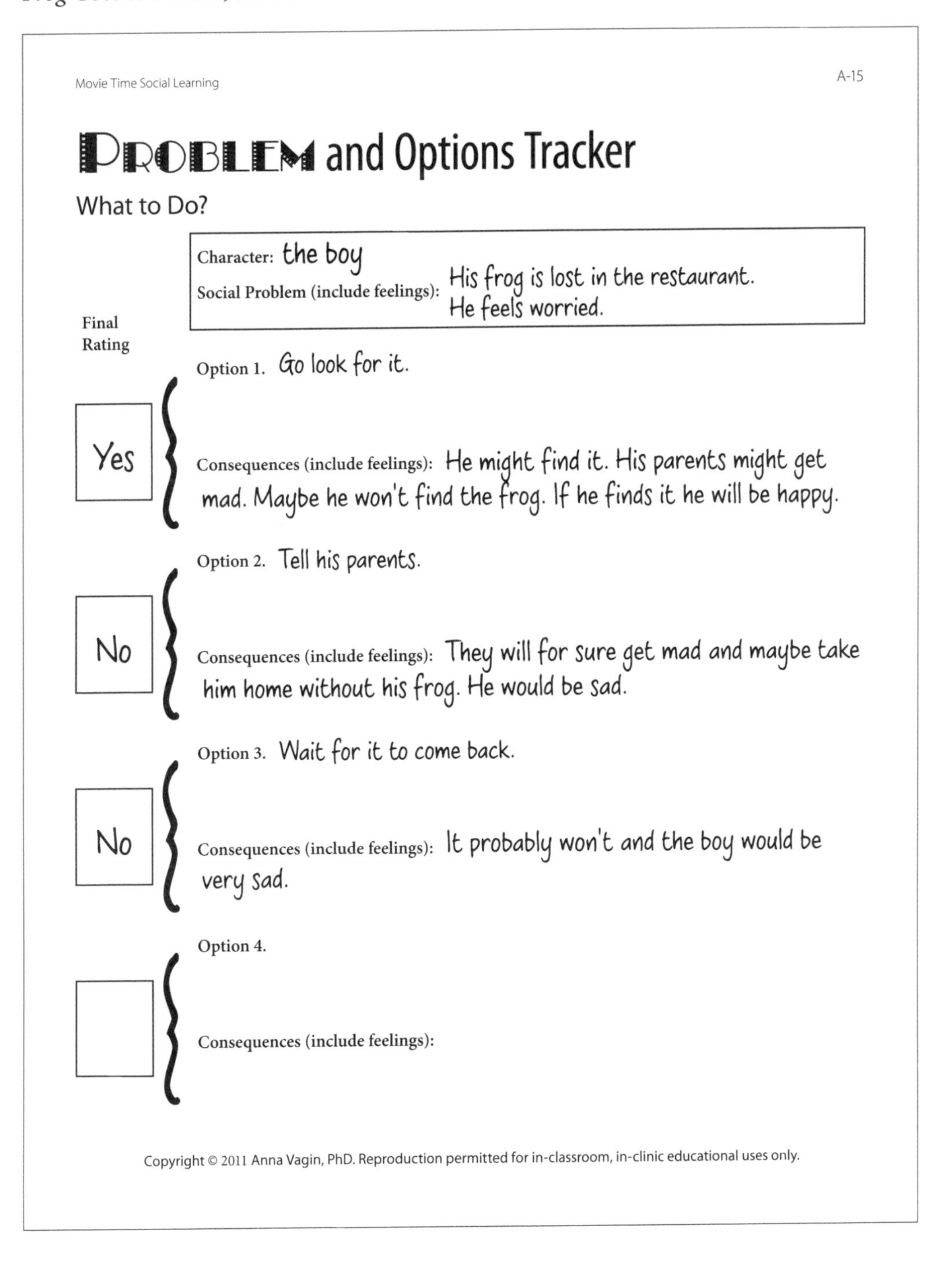

Movie Time Social Learning A-15

PROBLEM and Options Tracker

What to Do?

Character: the boy

Social Problem (include feelings): His frog is lost in the restaurant. He feels worried.

Final Rating

Yes — Option 1. Go look for it.

Consequences (include feelings): He might find it. His parents might get mad. Maybe he won't find the frog. If he finds it he will be happy.

No — Option 2. Tell his parents.

Consequences (include feelings): They will for sure get mad and maybe take him home without his frog. He would be sad.

No — Option 3. Wait for it to come back.

Consequences (include feelings): It probably won't and the boy would be very sad.

Option 4.

Consequences (include feelings):

Event and Feelings Tracker Template

Movie Time Social Learning

A-16

EVENT and Feelings Tracker

Example of a completed Event and Feelings Tracker for Moving Up Mindreaders, from *The Indian in the Cupboard*, Multiple Scenes.

Movie Time Social Learning A-17

EVENT and Feelings Tracker

Little Bear and Boone

Conjunctions Lists

Movie Time Social Learning

CONJUNCTIONS Lists

Conjunctions for Junior Mindreaders

Coordinating Conjunctions	Subordinating Conjunctions
and	because
but	if
so	

Conjunctions for Moving Up and Varsity Mindreaders

Coordinating Conjunctions	Subordinating Conjunctions		
and	after	even if	until
but	although	even though	when
or	as	if	whenever
for	as long as	since	where
so	because	so that	while
	before	unless	

Appendix B

Letters and Forms

The following sample letters and releases are included in this appendix:

- Movie Time Parent Information Letter
- Movie Time Movie Watching Release
- Movie Time Release to Video Record
- Allergy and Food Release (if you plan to serve snacks during movie watching)

You can customize these to fit the needs of your program.

Movie Time Parent Information Letter

Your letterhead here

Date

Dear ______________________________,

In my work with your child this year, I'll be using the therapeutic program Movie Time Social Learning (Vagin, 2012). Incorporating the ideas related to Social Thinking® (Winner, 2000), this program uses scenes from carefully selected children's movies to teach students important Social Thinking concepts. The activities in the program are meant to improve your child's ability to identify the thoughts, feelings, and plans of characters, understand and explain multiple perspectives, understand nonverbal information, empathize with others, and use more complex language.

Attached you will find a release form. Please fill it out and return it with your child as soon as possible. Be assured that the movies your child will be viewing are age-appropriate and used within the context of an interactive therapeutic program. We won't be "just watching a movie." Movies may include, but are not limited to, ______________________________. After we've started using the Movie Time Social Learning program, I'll be sending home activities for you to try with your child to reinforce the ideas we discuss in our work. Please feel free to call me with any questions or comments.

Thanks so much!

[***Your name here***]

Movie Watching Parental Release

Movie Time Social Learning B-2

Your Letterhead Here

Release to View Movies with Minor

Permission is hereby granted for [***your name here***] to show G-rated or not-rated movies to my child _________________________________ as part of his/her therapeutic intervention. I understand that [***your name here***] will use professional discretion in selecting movies for my child to see. Movie viewing may take place in individual and/or group sessions.

______ By initialing here, I give permission for my child to watch movies rated PG, if [***your name here***] believes that watching such movies would be therapeutically beneficial.

______ By initialing here, I give permission for my child to watch movies rated PG-13, if [***your name here***] believes that watching such movies would be therapeutically beneficial.

I understand that I may cancel this release at any time by stating my wish to [***your name here***].

_________________________________ (signed)

_________________________________ (relationship to child)

_________________________________ (printed)

_________________________________ (date)

Please contact me with any questions.

Movie Time Release to Video Record

Your Letterhead Here

Release to Video Record

Permission is hereby granted for [***your name here***] to video record my child ______________________. I understand that this may take place in individual and/or group sessions. I also give permission for recordings of my child to be reviewed and discussed during therapy sessions for educational purposes. I understand that recordings of my child will **not** be shown to other parents or professionals, and will not be published in any form.

I understand that I may cancel this release at any time by stating my wish to [***your name here***].

______________________ (signed)

______________________ (relationship to child)

______________________ (printed)

______________________ (date)

Movie Time Allergy and Food Release

Your Letterhead Here

Food can be a useful tool during Movie Time Social Learning therapeutic sessions, whether it's used as a sequenced social cooking activity, an outing by pairs of students to purchase one item together, while watching a movie, or a treat for a job well done. Please alert us to any food restrictions or allergies in the box below. Thank you.

I give permission for my child ____________________ to eat during therapy sessons with [***your name here***]. Food may include popcorn, candy, gum, juice, cookies, or pizza.

Food Allergies and Restrictions

My child is allergic to:	I strongly prefer that my child not eat:

I understand that I may cancel this release at any time by stating my wish to [***your name here***].

______________________________ (signed)

______________________________ (relationship to child)

______________________________ (printed)

______________________________ (date)

Appendix C

Resources and References

This appendix includes suggested movies for Movie Time Social Learning as well as picture books, games and toys, and other resources to use with students as they develop their social thinking skills. The book's references are also included.

Movies

The movies referred to in this book generally are easy to find; all were released between 2000 and 2009. Many are available at local libraries or video rental stores. Some can be viewed directly on YouTube or Netflix.

Movies for Junior Mindreaders:

- *Frog Goes to Dinner* (Scholastic Video Collection)
- *Knuffle Bunny* (Scholastic Storybook Treasures)
- *No Roses for Harry* (Scholastic Video Collection)
- *Whistle for Willie* (Scholastic Video Collection)

Movies for Moving Up Mindreaders:

- *The Indian in the Cupboard,* rated PG (Columbia TriStar Home Entertainment)
- *Like Mike,* rated PG (Twentieth Century Fox Film Corporation)

Movie for Varsity Mindreaders:

- *Harry Potter and the Order of the Phoenix,* rated PG-13 (Warner Home Video)

Additional movies:

- *Akeelah and the Bee*, rated PG (Lions Gate Films)
- *Diary of a Wimpy Kid*, rated PG (20th Century Fox)
- *Finding Nemo*, rated G (Walt Disney Studios Home Entertainment)
- *Fly Away Home,* rated PG (Sony Pictures Home Entertainment)
- *The Pink Panther,* rated PG (Sony Pictures Home Entertainment)
- *Pooh's Grand Adventure: The Search for Christopher Robin* (Buena Vista Home Entertainment)
- *The Red Balloon* (Janus Films)
- *Shrek,* rated PG (DreamWorks Home Entertainment)
- *Sylvester and the Magic Pebble* (Scholastic Video Collection)

Book Recommendations

There are many wonderful children's books to use when working on social thinking with Junior and Moving Up Mindreaders. Pictures provide a visual support for children as they work to identify thoughts, feelings, and plans.

These are some of the features I look for when selecting a book to support work on social thinking:

- Clear pictures, not too "artsy" or abstract
- Pictures that support the storyline
- Pictures that show clear facial expression
- Story lines that are within the realm of experience of the child (not too fantastical)
- Stories that show a range of feeling states as well as changes in feeling states

The following are some recommended picture books for Junior and Moving Up Mindreaders:

- *Duck in the Truck* by Jez Alborough
- *Fly Guy* (series) by Tedd Arnold
- *In the Town All Year 'Round* by Rotraut Susanne Berner
- *The Chocolate-Covered-Cookie Tantrum* by Deborah Blumenthal
- *Hunter's Best Friend at School* (series) by Laura Malone Elliott
- *Tiger Can't Sleep* by S.J. Fore
- *Wemberly Worried* by Kevin Henkes
- *Rosie's Walk* by Pat Hutchins
- *My Lucky Day* by Keiko Kasza
- *The Pig's Picnic* by Keiko Kasza
- *Where Is the Cake?* by T.T. Khing
- *Where Is the Cake Now?* By T.T. Khing
- *Frog and Toad* (series) by Arnold Lobel
- *Katie and the Dinosaurs* by James Mayhew
- *All in One Piece* by Jill Murphy
- *Five Minutes' Peace* by Jill Murphy
- *Peace at Last* by Jill Murphy
- *Beatrice Doesn't Want To* by Laura Numeroff
- *Sam's Sandwich* by David Pelham
- *Dragon Gets By* (series) by Dav Pilkey
- *Good Night, Gorilla* by Peggy Rathmann
- *Curious George Rides a Bike* by H.A. Rey
- *Duck! Rabbit!* by Amy Krouse Rosenthal and Tom Lichtenheld
- *Who Will Tuck Me in Tonight?* by Carol Roth
- *Mr. Putter and Tabby* (series) by Cynthia Rylant

- *The True Story of the 3 Little Pigs!* by Jon Scieszka
- *He Came with the Couch* by David Slonim
- *Sylvester and the Magic Pebble* by William Steig
- *Pigsty* by Mark Teague
- *The Circus Ship* by Chris Van Dusen
- *Lucky Duck* by Ellen Weiss
- *Elephant and Piggie* (series) by Mo Willems
- *Mouse and Mole* (series) by Wong Herbert Yee

Game and Toy Recommendations

For younger children:

- Cariboo — Cranium
- Feed the Kitty — Gamewright
- Fill 'er Up — Gamewright
- Go Away Monster! — Gamewright
- I Spy Eagle Eye — Briarpatch
- The Ladybug Game — Zobmondo!!
- Penguin Pile-Up — Ravensburger
- Silly Socks (Chimp & Zee) — Pressman
- Sneaky Bunnies (Chimp & Zee) — Pressman
- Snail's Pace Race — Ravensburger
- Teddy Mix & Match — Ravensburger
- Thomas' Tracks & Trestles Game — Briarpatch

Elementary school age and up:

- Apples to Apples — Mattel
- Blokus — Strata Gems
- Exago — Goliath
- Eureka! — Gamewright
- Forbidden Island (cooperative game) — Gamewright
- Gobblet! — Blue Orange Games
- In a Pickle — Gamewright
- Monster Maker — Buffalo Games
- Race to the Roof — Ravensburger
- Rivers, Roads & Rails — Ravensburger
- Sabotauer — Z Man Games
- Should I or Shouldn't I? What Would Others Think? — Social Thinking
- Sort It Out! — University Games
- Stratego — Milton Bradley
- Trapdoor Checkers — Goliath
- Up the River — Ravensburger
- Whoonu — Cranium
- Zigity — Cranium

Movement/sensory input:

- Ernest the Balancing Bear — Schylling (eBay)
- Play-Doh materials
- Team Walker — Weplay
- Twister — Milton Bradley
- Zoom Ball — eBay, therapy catalogs

Construction/technology:

- Kapla building sets
- Marble run building sets
- Mindflex — Mattel
- Rokenbok toys
- Rube Goldberg building projects (e.g., "This Too Shall Pass" and "The Cog" on YouTube)

Additional Resources and Materials

Some marvelous interactive software programs are available to build understanding of emotions.

For younger children:

- Basic Emotion Recognition™ interactive software (2011). http://www.linguisystems.com
- The Transporters by Simon Baron-Cohen, Jonathan Drori, Claire Harcup, and Nicholas Paske (2009) [DVD]. London, UK: Changing Media Development Ltd. http://www.thetransporters.com
- You Are a Social Detective! Interactive CD by Pamela J. Crooke and Michelle Garcia Winner (2011). http://www.socialthinking.com

For older children:

- Mind Reading: The Interactive Guide to Emotions by Simon Baron-Cohen (2007, v. 1.3) [CD-ROM]. University of Cambridge: Jessica Kingsley Publishers. http://www.jkp.com/catalogue/book/Mind_Reading_sit

Many books and materials are available through Social Thinking Publishing, (www.socialthinking.com) as well as other publishers to help children develop social cognitive awareness.

For younger children:

- The Kimochis™ line, providing stuffed friends, books, and a curriculum for social emotional development. San Rafael CA: Plushy Feely Corp. http://kimochis.com
- *You Are a Social Detective! Explaining Social Thinking to Kids* by Pamela J. Crooke and Michelle Garcia Winner (2008). San Jose, CA: Social Thinking Publishing
- *Superflex®: A Superhero Social Thinking Curriculum* by Stephanie Madrigal and Michelle Garcia Winner (2008). San Jose, CA: Social Thinking Publishing
- *We Can Make It Better!* by Elizabeth M. Delsandro (2010). San Jose, CA: Social Thinking Publishing

For older children:

- *Jarvis Clutch — Social Spy* by Mel Levine (2001). Cambridge, MA: Educators Publishing Service.
- *Social Fortune or Social Fate: A Social Thinking Graphic Novel Map for Social Quest Seekers* by Pamela Crooke and Michelle Garcia Winner (2010). San Jose, CA: Social Thinking Publishing
- *Socially Curious and Curiously Social: A Social Thinking Guidebook for Bright Teens & Young Adults* by Pamela J. Crooke and Michelle Garcia Winner (2009). San Jose, CA: Social Thinking Publishing

Additionally, many materials are available to assist with regulation:

- Child-size zafu (meditation) cushions: http://www.sittingstill.com or stores selling yoga or meditation supplies
- Fidgets, bumpy seating cushions, mouth toys: http://www.southpawenterprises.com or http://www.abilitations.com
- Story Grammar Marker® program by Maryellen Rooney Moreau (1991). Springfield, MA: MindWing Concepts, Inc. http://www.mindwingconcepts.com
- Time Timer: http://www.timetimer.com
- Zoom Ball: Most readily available on eBay
- *The Zones of Regulation®* by Leah Kuypers (2011). San Jose, CA: Social Thinking Publishing. http://www.socialthinking.com
- To reach Anna Vagin, PhD, and learn about her practice and current work: http://www.socialtime.org

References

Baron-Cohen, S. (1995). *Mindblindness: An essay on autism and theory of mind.* Cambridge, MA: MIT Press.

Baron-Cohen, S. (2007). *Mind reading: The interactive guide to emotions (v. 1.3)* [CD-ROM]. London, England: Jessica Kingsley Publishers.

Brown, P., & Levinson, S. (1987). *Politeness: Some universals in language usage.* Cambridge, UK: Cambridge University Press.

Crooke, P. J., Hendrix, R. E., & Rachman, J. Y. (2008). Brief report: Measuring the effectiveness of teaching social thinking to children with Asperger syndrome (AS) and high functioning autism (HFA). *Journal of Autism and Developmental Disorders, 38*(3), 581-591. DOI: 10.1007/s10803-007-0466-1.

Dunn Buron, K. & Curtis, M. (2003). *The incredible 5-point scale.* Shawnee Mission, KS: Autism Asperger Publishing Co.

Ekman, P. (2007). *Emotions revealed: Recognizing faces and feelings to improve communication and emotional life* (2nd ed.). New York, NY: Henry Holt and Co.

Feuerstein, R. (2000). Mediated learning experience, instrumental enrichment, and the learning propensity assessment device. In *Clinical Practice Guidelines* (pp. 557-577). Bethesda MD: The Interdisciplinary Council on Developmental and Learning Disorders. Retrieved from http://www.icdl.com/graduate/documents/Chapter22.pdf

Goldin-Meadow, S. (2003). *Hearing gesture: how our hands help us think.* Cambridge, MA: Harvard University Press.

Goldin-Meadow, S. (2004). Gesture's role in the learning process. *Theory Into Practice, 43*(4) 314-321.

Goleman, D. (2006). *Social intelligence: The revolutionary new science of human relationships.* New York, NY: Bantam Books.

Gray, C. (2005). Foreword. In Howley, M. & Arnold, E., *Revealing the hidden social code: Social stories for people with autistic spectrum disorders.* London, England: Jessica Kingsley Publishers.

Greenspan, S. I. & Weider, S. (2000). Developmentally appropriate interactions and practices. In *Clinical Practice Guidelines* (pp. 261-281). Bethesda, MD: The Interdisciplinary Council on Developmental and Learning Disorders. Retrieved from http://www.icdl.com/graduate/documents/Chapter12.pdf

Grice, H. P. (1975). Logic and conversation. In P. Cole & J. Morgan (Eds.), *Syntax and Semantics, 3*, 41-58. New York, NY: Academic Press.

Hymes, D. (1972). On communicative competence. In J.B. Pride & J. Holmes (Eds.), *Sociolinguistics: Selected readings* (pp. 269-293). Harmondsworth, England: Penguin Books.

Kuhn, T. (1962). *The structure of scientific revolutions.* Chicago, IL: University of Chicago Press.

Kuypers, L. (2011). *The zones of regulation.* San Jose, CA: Think Social Publishing, Inc.

Leech, G. (1983). *Principles of pragmatics.* New York, NY: Longman Linguistics Library.

Madrigal, S., & Winner, M. G. (2008). *Superflex® … A superhero social thinking curriculum.* San Jose, CA: Think Social Publishing, Inc.

McAfee, J. (2002). *Navigating the social world.* Arlington, Texas: Future Horizons, Inc.

McGinn, C. (2005). *The power of movies: How screen and mind interact.* New York, NY: Pantheon Books.

Peters, A. M. (1983). *The units of language acquisition: Monographs in applied psycholinguistics.* Cambridge, England: Cambridge University Press.

Prutting, C. A., & Kirchner, D. M. (1987). A clinical appraisal of the pragmatic aspects of language. *Journal of Speech and Hearing Disorders, 52*, 105-119.

Rapee, R., Wignall, A., Spence, S., Cobham, V., & Lyneham, H. (2000). *Helping your anxious child.* Oakland, CA: New Harbinger Publications, Inc.

Sameroff, A., & Chandler, M. (1975). Reproductive risk and the continuum of caretaking casualty. In F. Horowitz (Ed.), *Review of child development research.* Chicago, IL: University of Chicago Press, *4*, 187-244.

Schiefelbusch, R. L., & Pickar, J. (Eds.). (1984). *The acquisition of communicative competence.* Baltimore: University Park Press.

Snider, E. D. (2010, June 8). What's the big deal?: *Breathless* (1960). Retrieved from http://www.film.com/movies

Stern. D. (1985). *The interpersonal world of the infant.* New York, NY: Basic Books.

Vagin, A. (1997). *Interaction patterns in cleft palate babies and their mothers.* (Unpublished doctoral dissertation.) University of California at Berkeley, Berkeley, CA, and San Francisco State University, San Francisco, CA.

Winner, M. G. (2000). *Inside out: What makes a person with social cognitive deficits tick?* San Jose, CA: Think Social Publishing, Inc.

Winner, M. G. (2005). *Think social! A social thinking curriculum for school-age students.* San Jose, CA: Think Social Publishing, Inc.

Winner, M. G. (2002). *Thinking about you thinking about me.* San Jose, CA: Think Social Publishing, Inc.

Winner, M. G. (2005). *Worksheets! For teaching social thinking and related skills.* San Jose, CA: Think Social Publishing, Inc.

Winner, M. G. (2008). Social thinking: cognition to enhance communication and learning. In K. Dunn Buron & P. J. Wolfberg (Eds.), *Learners on the autism spectrum: Preparing highly qualified educators* (pp. 209-231). Shawnee Mission, KS: Autism Asperger Publishing Co.

Winner, M. G., & Crooke, P. J. (2008). *You are a social detective! Explaining social thinking to kids.* San Jose, CA: Think Social Publishing, Inc.

Winner, M. G., Crooke, P. J., & Madrigal, S. (2011). The social thinking–social communication profile.® Retrieved from http://www.socialthinking.com/what-is-social-thinking/social-thinking-social-communication-profile

Wolfberg, P. J. (1999). *Play & imagination in children with autism.* New York, NY: Teachers College Press.

Core Books About the Social Thinking Methodology & Related Teaching Strategies

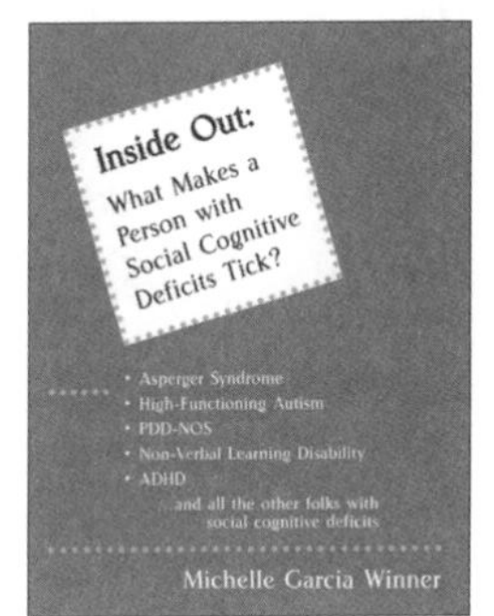

Inside Out: What Makes a Person with Social Cognitive Deficits Tick?

By Michelle Garcia Winner

For professionals and parents to use with all ages!

The starting place to learn about the ILAUGH Model upon which Social Thinking is based. Discusses the direct connection between social thinking and academic problems such as reading comprehension and written expression, and helps readers pinpoint specific challenges in a child or student. Valuable insight on information we expect students to know to become strong learners but that doesn't develop "naturally" in everyone.

Thinking About YOU Thinking About ME, 2nd Edition

By Michelle Garcia Winner

For professionals and parents to use with all ages!

Learn more about social interaction and social awareness! Explains Michelle Garcia Winner's core Social Thinking concepts and treatment methods, with extensive curriculum content on perspective taking as well as assessment using the Social Thinking Dynamic Assessment Protocol®. Age-targeted lesson and activity ideas, templates and handouts included. A precursor to using books like *Superflex, You Are A Social Detective,* and more!

Think Social! A Social Thinking Curriculum for School-Aged Students, 2nd Edition

By Michelle Garcia Winner

For parents and professionals to use with all ages!

A complement to *Thinking About YOU Thinking About ME,* this is the fundamental Social Thinking curriculum book to help individuals K-12 and into adulthood. The book sequences through eight chapters and 69 lessons that help students explore the basics of working and thinking in a group. Each chapter addresses how to use and interpret language (verbal and nonverbal) to further understand the context of communications.

Learn how **Movie Time Social Learning** is part of our larger Social Thinking Methodology

If you're just starting with Movie Time, know there is much more!

Help your students broaden their social competencies through the Social Thinking Methodology!

Extend your teaching about perspective taking, social observation, social self-regulation, the social-emotional chain reaction, executive functions and more.

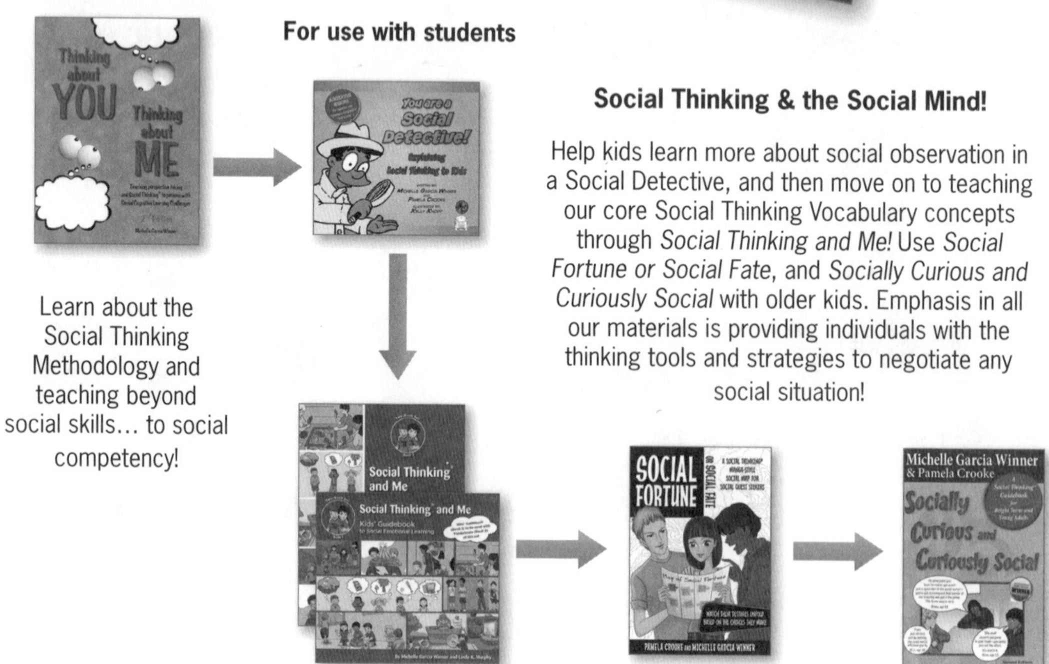

For Interventionists (Parents & Professionals)

Learn about the Social Thinking Methodology and teaching beyond social skills... to social competency!

For use with students

Social Thinking & the Social Mind!

Help kids learn more about social observation in a Social Detective, and then move on to teaching our core Social Thinking Vocabulary concepts through *Social Thinking and Me!* Use *Social Fortune or Social Fate*, and *Socially Curious and Curiously Social* with older kids. Emphasis in all our materials is providing individuals with the thinking tools and strategies to negotiate any social situation!

Find these and other books and teaching materials at www.SocialThinking.com